A Beautiful Season

Our Journey of Faith from Texas to Mozambique

Julie Henderson, DVM

Published in the USA by:
Julie Henderson DVM
www.cvmusa.org/hendersons

Printed in the United States of America
ISBN: 978-1-7324975-0-4 (paperback)
          978-1-7324975-1-1 (ebook)

This book is dedicated to Alegria and the
One who changed her mourning into joy.

Contents

Part I: **Calling and Preparation, February 2006–August 2010**

Acknowledgments

I COULD NOT HAVE WRITTEN *A Beautiful Season* without the help of my sweet mom and my dear friend, Sandra, both of whom gave invaluable feedback and continual encouragement. Thank you! I also want to thank Natalie Hanemann for her professional editing and personal encouragement.

Steve and I also owe a debt of gratitude to our many friends, family, and church congregations who held us up in prayer and gave financial support to the work in Mozambique. I hope this story will bless you as you have blessed us. We also want to thank our friends at Christian Veterinary Mission who gave us invaluable training, advice, and encouragement while looking after our physical, emotional, and spiritual health while on the field. Likewise, so many from our home congregation at Alpine were always there and always praying for us.

I want to thank Steve, my husband, my best friend and partner in this work. And we want to thank our brothers and sisters in Christ amongst the Yao people. Your faith and courage inspires us and your love for the lost fills us with joy. Our hearts will always be intertwined with yours. You are *Chinonyelo Cha Isa* (The Love of Jesus).

Above all, we give thanks to Jesus Christ, our Lord and Savior, who brought us together and prepared this beautiful work in advance for us to do. To Him be the glory!

Terms and Locations

Anganga: respected elder or grandmother

Arungu: westerner or white person

Chappa: (pronounced "shappa") public transport van

Chinonyelo Cha Isa: Chiyao for "The Love of Jesus," this became the name of the Nomba church.

Chiyao: the language spoken by Yao.

CSJ: Center for Social Justice, the community development resource center in the village founded by our teammates.

CVM: Christian Veterinary Mission, our sending agency based in Seattle, WA.

Dada: a familiar Yao term for "sister."

Good News for Africa: (aka *Boa Nova Para Africa*), the mission group in Mozambique to which we belonged.

Kuchijinji: the Anglican Diocese in Lichinga where we lived for the first year while building our home in the village.

Lichinga: a small city that is the capital of the province of Niassa in Northern Mozambique.

Machamba: cornfield, frequently beans are also grown as well, and occasionally other staple crops. They are usually located several kilometers from the village and during planting and harvest times, the family may live in a small hut on the property to avoid the cost of going back and forth.

Mamãe: Portuguese for "mama."

Maputo: the capital of Mozambique, located on the southern tip of the country.

MTI: Missions Training International is located in Palmer Lake, CO and is where we received language acquisition and cross-cultural training before we left, as well as debriefing when we returned.

Niassa: Chiyao word for "lake," specifically Lake Malawi, and the name of the province in Northern Mozambique where we worked.

Proclaimer: a solar-powered, audio version of the New Testament, made by Faith Comes by Hearing, available in many tribal languages including Chiyao.

SIM: an international mission organization in Mozambique to which the Talbots, Smiths, and Paetzolds belonged, as well as others not mentioned in this book.

Tia: Portuguese word for "aunt"

Unyago: Yao ceremony for initiating children into adulthood.

Xima: (pronounced "sheema") aka *ugadi*, the cornmeal-mush staple that is the foundation of every meal.

YWAM: Youth with a Mission, an international mission organization in Mozambique to which the Selemanis, Jon, Julio, and formerly the Van Steltons belonged as well as others not mentioned in this book.

Regional Map. Used with permission.

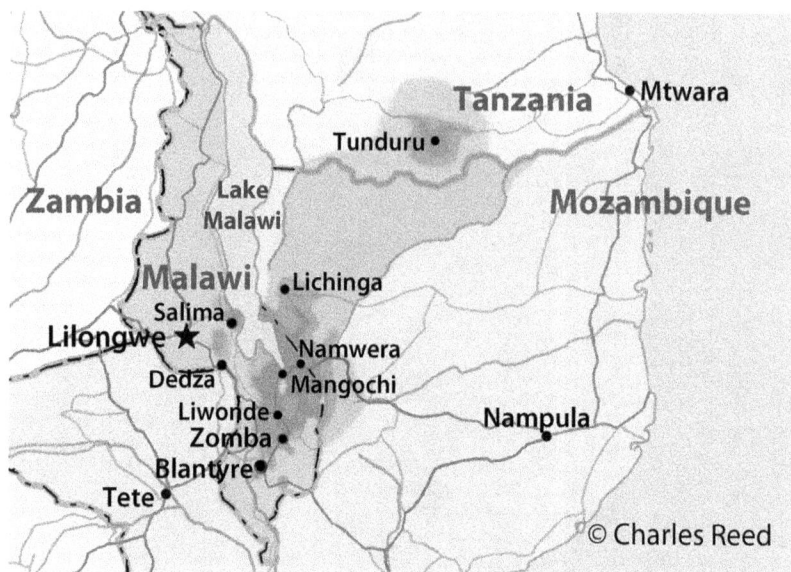

Map of Yao territory. Used with permission.

"WORSHIP IS GIVING GOD THE best that He has given you. Be careful what you do with the best you have. Whenever you get a blessing from God, give it back to Him as a love gift. Take time to meditate before God and offer the blessing back to Him in a deliberate act of worship. If you hoard it for yourself, it will turn into spiritual dry rot, as the manna did when it was hoarded. God will never allow you to keep a spiritual blessing completely for yourself. It must be given back to Him so that He can make it a blessing to others."[1]

---

[1]   Taken from *My Utmost for His Highest®* by Oswald Chambers, edited by James Reimann, © 1992 by Oswald Chambers Publications Assn., Ltd., and used by permission of Discovery House, Grand Rapids MI 49501. All rights reserved.

Foreword

HAVE YOU EVER CONSIDERED LEAVING your family, friends, and possessions to travel to a foreign nation and learn a new language and culture, in order to obey Jesus' command in Matthew 28?

If so, I encourage you to take this journey first with Julie. Even if you haven't considered such a bold step, take this journey anyway. You'll return with even deeper convictions. Julie and her husband Steve share a deep passion for obeying Jesus' command to "Go . . . and make disciples of all nations . . ."

Having accompanied her to Mozambique on one of her return trips and reading *A Beautiful Season*, I had to take a serious look at my own journey, realizing my so-called commitment to Christ and trust in God fell woefully short. Julie shows us what commitment, courage, sacrifice, and trust in God truly look like. She made me want to be a better person.

Reading *A Beautiful Season* made me face up to just how halfhearted my commitment to God and my discipleship effort have been. No doubt you will reexamine your passion and your faith will be strengthened as well. This is a story of God's bottomless love for the "unreached." It is also a story of steadfast friendships, surprising betrayals, suffering, and heroism using vibrant language that makes the people on the pages come alive.

I cried, I laughed, and I reflected many times as I journeyed with Julie to get to know the Yao people of Mozambique. From this predominantly Muslim tribe, you will meet people who not only left family, friends, and possessions to become Christ-followers, but they were also faced with the real threat of death. I must warn you that you will likely think of them when tempted to slip into the habit of complaining about *anything*! I often do.

Reading this book also helped me reshape the way I look at consumption, conservation, sacrifice, and brotherly love—especially love for people who either have not heard or not welcomed the Good News.

Read it.

Sandra Brumbaugh
Missions Committee Member, Alpine Church of Christ
January 15, 2018

Part I: Calling and Preparation
February 2006–August 2010

Chapter 1

"Blessed are the poor in spirit . . ."
—*Matthew 5:3*

Uganda, February 2006

EVERYTHING CHANGED IN A MOMENT, *that* moment . . .

Dusk was settling in as I sat in the back of the old school bus. It was crammed full of children, parked on a busy dirt road on the outskirts of Kampala. The dusty air had been tolerably warm when the bus was bumping along the road with all the windows pushed down. But once we came to a stop, it became stale and suffocating.

I tried to push back panicky thoughts of claustrophobia by focusing my attention on Rachel, who was sitting next to me. She seemed exceedingly content in her yellow taffeta dress. It was about two sizes too small so that the top two buttons in the back had to be left undone. I asked if she was hot in that scratchy dress. She said no, on the contrary, she still felt cool after spending most of the afternoon in the pool. She had a dreamy smile on her face when she spoke of it.

It was the first time Rachel had ever been in a pool. The first time, in fact, she had ever journeyed outside her village in cen-

1

tral Uganda. Rachel was one of the millions of children in Sub-Saharan Africa orphaned by AIDS. After losing both parents, she was being raised by her aging grandmother. Within a few short years, their roles would reverse. Rachel would become her grandmother's caretaker as she lay on her deathbed. At only nine years of age, Rachel knew more about grief and loss than I had learned in forty-three years.

I pondered this for a moment. Then, reaching into my bag, I took out a roll of Sweet-tarts and placed it into her hands. I expected her to gobble them up, but instead, her expression became solemn as she carefully unwrapped the candy. She took out two pieces at a time and placed them oh so carefully into the black velvet pouch tied around her neck.

"Two for my sister. Two for my brother," she said as she reached in again. Another two went in for someone else. Then, she turned to her teacher and gave him two. Finally, she placed the last two in her mouth, and her solemn expression changed back into the dreamy smile. I wanted to tell her that I had a whole bunch of candies that I planned to leave with her at the end of our visit. Something checked me, however, and I said nothing. I thought about how her perspective on life was so different from my own. It was *her* perspective that was pleasing to God and not my own. It was in *that very moment* God began to transform my stony heart to one of flesh.

A scripture flashed to the forefront of my mind. "Blessed are the poor in spirit, for theirs is the kingdom of heaven" (Matt. 5:3). Suddenly, the beatitude verses that always seemed so abstract and lofty to me became real. Rachel possessed the kingdom, but I had somehow missed it.

Chapter 2

"As for the proud one, his soul is not
right within him." —Habakkuk 2:4

"Take it easy on me, Dr. Julie," Deidre said. "I've had *such* a hard day. I had to take Aubrey all the way to Dallas to have her hair done and it cost me two hundred dollars!"

Isn't there anyone around here who can cut her hair? For Pete's sake, she is twelve years old, I thought.

"Really?" I said as I looked over her horse's record.

As my client continued to list off a steady stream of recent trials, all of which involved large sums of money, we walked outside to her horse. He was a handsome chestnut gelding with a pleasant expression and a kind but weary eye. He was waiting patiently for us while tied up to a shiny aluminum gooseneck horse trailer, which was hooked up to a late-model, one-ton pickup truck. The crux of the problem, it seemed from my client's perspective, was that her daughter got second place instead of first at the last horse show. So, naturally, something must be wrong with the horse.

She continued giving me all the details of her trials while I quietly surveyed the horse, truck, and trailer. They were easily worth a small fortune—it was a nice rig, and he was a quality show horse (a saint, really). He was a kind, reliable mount that would do his job in the show ring regardless of the expertise or temperament of the jockey. Aubrey had a bad temper, I knew, because I had seen it. She usually blamed the horse if things didn't go just right.

My mind flashed back to Rachel, as I had just returned from Uganda the previous day. I thought about how pleased she had been with her Sweet-tarts, and how eager she was to share them with her siblings and teacher.

"What am I doing with my life?" I thought. *"Am I making any difference?"*

"Sure, Deidre," I responded when she finished her story. "I'll take it easy on you. Sounds like you've had it pretty rough lately. Let's take a look at him and see what could be the problem."

I loved horses, and I loved my job, but I have to confess I didn't always love the people that came with the horses. Most of my clients were wonderful, caring people who shared my passion for horses. But my first day back from Africa, I didn't see one of *those* clients; I saw Deidre.

The year 2006 marked a turning point in the trajectory of my life. I had spent only twelve days in Uganda, but the trip affected me greatly. It was my first experience getting a close-up look at poverty. I wanted to talk about it with everybody, but nobody seemed very interested in the children or the poverty. They just wanted to know what wild animals I had seen.

Suddenly, I found myself questioning the relevance of the career I had worked so hard to build. I am an equine surgeon. It took eleven years of university studies, multiple degrees, and certification examinations in preparation to qualify. That was followed by many years of hard work in private practice to build a good reputation. I had helped a lot of horses, but what had I done of significance in the kingdom of God? And what about all the kids like Rachel?

Deidre served as a mirror for my heart that day. When I compared my reflection to Deidre's and Rachel's, I came to the painful realization that the condition of my heart was closer to Deidre's.

Chapter 3

"I will give you a new heart and put a new spirit within you . . ." —Ezekiel 36:26

I DECIDED TO BECOME AN advocate volunteer for Compassion International, the organization through which my husband Steve and I sponsored Rachel and other children. When I planned the Uganda trip, I thought it would be a once-in-a-lifetime trip for me. I had wanted to go to Africa since I was a child and saw the movie *Born Free*. I was mystified by the very thought of it. We also sponsored two children there, so I thought it would be a great opportunity to see how well the ministry worked. The trip, however, changed my entire perspective on life. As for the ministry, it far exceeded even my lofty expectations.

I came back on fire for the ministry, wishing we had the resources to sponsor a hundred kids. Since we didn't, I thought being an advocate for the ministry was the next best thing. Maybe I could convince one hundred people to each sponsor one child. That was my goal. It turned out to be much harder than I'd expected. Most people did not want to hear about poverty. I couldn't understand why. I still don't understand why, almost ten years later. Most people would rather talk about almost anything else than children living in poverty. Even my husband, who fully supported our child sponsorships and my work in the ministry, didn't seem too interested. And he is a good and kind man, always looking for opportunities to share Christ with people.

The following year, in 2007, Compassion was organizing a trip to India, where we sponsored a little girl named Tami. I had to find a way to go on that trip because I had been praying that I could meet all our sponsored kids face-to-face one day. I really, really wanted Steve to go with me so he could experience firsthand God's heart for the poor like I had in Uganda.

"Honey, I only have two weeks for vacation and there are places I haven't seen yet in America," Steve said. "Besides, a trip to India costs too much."

It was true. Steve had grown up on a ranch in Oklahoma and rarely had the opportunity to travel because of the livestock. He had never been east of the Mississippi River when we married. He had never seen our nation's capital, and he greatly desired a trip to the historic cities and battlefields of the eastern states for his next vacation.

"Okay," I replied with a sigh. "I won't bug you about it anymore."

I quietly resolved not to bring up the subject again. I was trying to be a better Christian and that meant being a better wife as well. I decided to pray about it. Hard as it was for me, we didn't talk about it again. I was so disappointed about the disconnect in our relationship that I had to pray a lot, every day for about a month, to get any peace about it. Then it happened. On the day of the deadline to reserve a spot for the India trip, Steve woke up that morning and turned to me and said, "I am going to India."

"Really?" I smiled and said a silent "thank you" to God. "I'll check and see if there are any places left open."

Steve never explained what changed his mind except that he woke up that morning with a great peace about going to India. He knew he needed to go. Whatever happened that night, it marked the beginning of a new stage in our life together. Although we had married several years earlier, up to that time, it was as if we were going through life on parallel tracks, close but never merging. He had his career and I had mine; sometimes we compared notes but never with true understanding of each other.

Even our hobbies, though similar in that we both enjoyed the outdoors, were also different. For a wedding present, Steve gave me a large back pack, and I gave him a horse. On our first backpacking trip into the beautiful Weminuche wilderness in Colorado, lugging that pack up the mountain, I found myself thinking the trip would be so much better if we had some pack mules.

But in India, God gently placed us on the same track. India, with its mass of human suffering, affected Steve in much the same way Uganda had affected me. We were both irreversibly changed, heading down a new track, to where, we had not a clue.

Chapter 4

"'Not by might nor by power, but by
My Spirit,' says the LORD of hosts."
—*Zechariah 4:6*

WE STARTED LOOKING FOR WAYS to serve in short-term missions. At a veterinary conference in Seattle, I thought we had stumbled on the perfect solution. Steve and I attended an evening seminar hosted by Christian Veterinary Mission. CVM is a mission-sending organization for veterinarians and their spouses who use veterinary medicine as a means to reach the lost in remote areas around the globe. The topic that night was about their mission outreach to nomadic Buddhist herders in Mongolia. The speaker was asking for volunteers to go on shuttle trips to Mongolia in the month of August when the people had their traditional endurance horse race, which frequently resulted in many equine fatalities. He also mentioned the construction of a new facility at the university where instructors were needed to teach equine surgery.

Wow, what a perfect fit! I thought. I could take off a couple weeks in the month of August. It was a relatively slow month in equine practice in Texas because breeding and foaling season was over. Additionally, not many people were going to horse shows because of the sweltering heat.

We waited for a chance to talk to the speaker after the presentation. When I got the chance, I tapped him on the shoulder and said, "We'd like to speak with you more about volunteering."

He smiled and turned to Steve and said, "Great! What kind of practice do you have?"

Steve, somewhat embarrassed for me, replied that he was a machinist, not a veterinarian, but that I was. I introduced myself and told him I was an equine surgeon and would like to go next August. The man's smile faded and his brow furrowed. "I'm sorry, but the tribal men would never accept a woman as a teacher."

"Neither did the Texas cowboys until they saw my work," I countered with a smile.

But the man wouldn't budge. It would hurt the ministry, or so he believed.

Ouch! A giant door slammed in my face. I hadn't felt that in many years, since I owned my own practice. As a child of the seventies, accustomed to breaking through glass ceilings, my first instinct was to fight, to push my way through that closed door, like I had done many times before to get where I was. In the early nineties, equine surgery was still very much a man's world. But again, something checked me. So I said, "Okay, let me know if you change your mind," but I knew he wouldn't.

Despite that initial letdown, Steve and I continued to seek God. We applied to join the pool of volunteers for short-term missions with Christian Veterinary Mission. In 2008, we went on a trip to Burkina Faso in West Africa through CVM. It was a whirlwind trip. We worked cattle out in the bush in an outreach to the nomadic Fulani, a Muslim tribal people considered an "unreached" people group. "Unreached" is a term used to describe a people group who did not yet have an indigenous church that could reach out to its own, thus necessitating foreign missionaries to lay the groundwork for pioneer church-planting efforts.

Wrestling cattle in a thorn corral seemed more like an African rodeo than a mission outreach, but we had fun. I am certain we provided great amusement to the Fulani. But when the night enveloped our campsite, as we sat out under the brilliant stars, the people came to hear the stories. The darkness was so thick and inky. You couldn't see your own hand in front of your face, yet I perceived there were many people around us. Rick, our host, chatted easily with them in Fulanji. We didn't know what was being said, but I had a great sense of peace and wonder as I listened to the rhythm of the conversation and gazed at the constellations of the southern sky.

Steve and I returned to Texas physically exhausted and emotionally drained. We hadn't had time to talk about everything during the trip. It wasn't until a few days after our return, as we sat out on our veranda at dusk, that we began to process the experience. Steve had kept a log and we started comparing notes on thoughts, emotions, and impressions we had at the different phases of our trip. The amazing thing was that we both came back from that journey feeling the call to long-term missions. We were on the same track even though we hadn't spoken to each other about it. God was calling us together down a path of uncertainty that would require more trust in Him. We took the fact that we both felt the *same* call as a sign that it was, indeed, from God and not some crazy whim.

We agreed that God was calling us to serve—but where? I thought maybe Burkina was the place, but Steve didn't have peace with that. Indeed, it wasn't long before the mission opportunity open to us in Burkina fell apart for various reasons. Another door shut. But this time I knew God was in it. I wasn't perturbed as I had been before because I knew what to do—pray and wait. So that is what we did, together. About six months later, another door was flung wide open and we walked through!

Chapter 5

"Wherever I am, there will
My servant be also . . ."
—*John 12:26, AMP*

THAT SUMMER A MISSIONARY FAMILY supported by our home congregation returned to America on furlough. They had been working in Niassa, the northern most province of Mozambique, with the Yao people. We invited them to dinner, hoping to learn more about the work. We were surprised and delighted to discover that they, having already heard from others about our interest in missions, were hoping to recruit us. We were ready to commit to join their team that same night, but they wisely insisted we plan a survey trip first to make sure it was a good fit.

We planned a trip for the following March 2009, to Lichinga, the capital of Niassa province. It was quite a journey to get there, and we traveled separately. Steve went the more direct route. Upon arrival to the Atlanta International Airport, it was a sixteen-hour direct flight to Johannesburg, South Africa. After spending the night in Johannesburg, he boarded another plane to Blantyre, Malawi.

I had departed twelve days earlier with another Compassion trip to Rwanda. I went to visit a girl named Neeza who we sponsored, as well as a young man my parents sponsored. Because there was no direct flight from Rwanda to Blantyre, I had booked a series of flights from Rwanda to Blantyre the day after the Rwanda tour ended. In theory, we were supposed to arrive in Blantyre within a few hours of one another. Our future teammate, Thomas, would meet us, and we would begin the eight-hour drive across Malawi and on to Mozambique.

It all seemed great on my itinerary, but as I waved good-bye to my friends from the trip—their smiling faces fading into the distance—fear and doubt crept in. What was I thinking? Would the flights all work out? Would I make all the connections? This is Africa, not America, and that doesn't even happen in America anymore. I don't know a soul here. I don't have a cell phone that works in Africa. I don't have a number for Thomas or know how to send a text message. How would I contact anyone if I missed a flight? Where would I stay? I must have been crazy to plan this trip.

It was about four p.m. My flight out of Kigali was to depart at four a.m., with a two-a.m. check-in time. Full of doubts and fear, I went back to my room and read a passage from a devotional book and then prayed. "Dear Lord, please let me know I am safe with You. Send me a friend to talk to while I prepare for the next part of the journey. You did send me here, didn't you?"

I went downstairs to the hotel restaurant and sat at an empty table. Looking around, I noticed a young woman looking at me. When our eyes met, she smiled warmly and said, "Why are you sitting alone? Come sit with me." I did, and as we dined together, she shared her story with me. She had survived the genocide in Rwanda because she was away at boarding school. She returned home only to find that her entire family had been murdered except for her mother. After witnessing the slaughter of her children, however, her mother had gone insane. As I listened to her story of tragedy, redemption, and faith, my own faith strengthened. The fear melted away and peace settled in my heart. I knew that God, in His infinite patience and understanding, had heard my prayer and answered it.

The rest of the journey was smooth. A taxi driver named Moses drove me to the airport. All the flights connected! Amazingly, Steve made it to Blantyre within a few hours of me, as planned, and we began the drive to Mozambique. Since that time, I am convinced when God calls us, He will make the way. He will go ahead of us and prepare a place for us, and we will find Him there.

Sometimes we have this crazy idea that we are bringing God, as if on a platter, and presenting Him to a lost people like the Yao, as if God hasn't yet made it to Northern Mozambique. While it is true the vast majority in that area has never heard the Good News of Jesus Christ and is perishing, it is also true that *He* has gone before us. *He* prepares the way and prepares hearts. *His* work is evident all around us if we will only look and see it. One of my greatest joys in working with the Yao was discovering the presence of God already there in the midst of them and within them.

Our two weeks in the village of Nomba with Thomas and Marie Hampton flew by. Soon we were on our way back home, together this time. God did allow us to be tested a bit on the trip. Steve's biggest fear about living in Mozambique was deadly snakes, namely the dreaded black mamba. My biggest fear was rats. We had close encounters with both on that trip.

We stayed in the house adjacent to the Hampton's. It was a

beautiful cob house with a steep thatched roof like theirs that belonged to the other missionary family on the team. They were in the States on furlough during our visit. I think the house had been empty for some time before our arrival. Unfortunately, it had become thoroughly infested with rats, *big* rats. There was one rat in particular that really got on my nerves, because he hung out in the pantry where the water filter was. Every time I went to get a drink of water, he would brazenly scamper past me despite my banging on the door before entering, hoping to scare him into hiding.

Each night, I would hear the rats rustling through our luggage on the bedroom floor. I tried to convince myself that maybe they were only *mice*, and that our luggage would keep them occupied so they wouldn't come any closer to the bed. I put my hope in the mosquito net we were sleeping under. Maybe it would keep them out. I also stopped drinking water several hours before bedtime so I wouldn't have to get up during the night. Steve always falls asleep as soon as his head hits the pillow. He wasn't the least concerned about either the pantry dweller or the late- night soirées in our luggage.

Then it happened. One night I was having one of those dreams that crossover into reality. In my dream I was standing at a long narrow table covered with a white cloth when right down the middle of the table, a large rat bounded past me. I felt something brush past my head and realized I was no longer dreaming; something really *had* brushed past my head. I jerked up and hit Steve a little harder than I intended. "Turn on the light!"

Annoyed at the rude awakening, Steve turned on his headlight just in time for me to see the rat going over the edge of the bed and on to the floor. Since I couldn't convince him to go rat killing at that hour, I insisted the light had to stay on the rest of the night. Unperturbed by the rat, but greatly perturbed by the light, Steve went to sleep on the couch in the den. I stayed awake in bed alone with my flashlight to protect me until dawn. That was undoubtedly the low point of the trip for me.

We did manage to trap a few rats before the trip was over. I wasn't swayed from my desire to live in the village, but resolved we would put a metal roof on our house (instead of the thatch) and definitely have a cat, maybe two.

A few days after the rat incident, we were walking single file on a narrow path through a cornfield to get to a man's fish pond. As we came out of the field, the path descended gradually into a bottom area that looked snaky. I regretted wearing sandals instead of boots. I noticed the lady directly in front of me was barefoot, which somehow comforted me. Steve was third in line after the owner of the pond and Thomas, then the barefoot woman, and I was fifth. Suddenly I heard shouting and a lot of commotion at the front of the procession. A mamba had crossed the path, gliding with lightning speed directly over the leader's foot! In what I later found to be typical Yao bravery, the man pursued the snake hoping to kill it with a rock, but it quickly vanished in the tall grass. It was a good reminder to watch our step and we both stayed on high alert for snakes for the rest of the trip.

Despite the mamba incident, Steve had the peace he was missing in Burkina. Once again, we were in agreement. This was the place God was calling us and the Yao were the people with whom He wanted us to share our lives. We thought highly of the work our teammates were doing in the village. We agreed the best way to bring the Good News to another person or people is through transforming relationships built on servant love. We couldn't wait to get started, but months of prayer and preparation lay ahead.

Chapter 6
Counting the Cost

AFTER RECEIVING THE BLESSING OF our church and our friends at Christian Veterinary Mission, we committed ourselves to five years of service in the mission field. It was a big step in faith for both of us, but we had prayed a lot and carefully counted the cost. We chose five years partly due to the age of our parents, who would be eighty years old by then, and partly because we believed we could honor a five-year commitment.

We realized we would not be able to retire by then, and it would not be easy to get back into the workforce at sixty years of age for Steve and fifty-two for myself. We knew it was foolish, from the worldly point of view, to leave our careers at that point in our lives. But we were also certain that was exactly what God was calling us to do. We also knew it would be difficult to separate from family, parents, children, and grandchildren. We had one granddaughter already and another one on the way. It was hard to think about not being a part of their lives for so many years.

People had mixed reactions about our plans. Some people were perplexed that a veterinarian and a machinist could qualify as missionaries. "What, are you going to preach to the animals?" as if the Great Commission (Matt. 28:19–20) was a calling only for seminary graduates. Steve got questions like, "Are you just going along because your wife wants to go?" To which he honestly replied, "If that was the reason I was going, I'd be making a big mistake."

The truth is, Steve is very much the spiritual leader of our family. He had been a serious student of the Bible his entire adult life, whereas I was a relative newcomer. As a young man, he'd graduated from a school of Bible and preaching and had never lost his heart for evangelism even though he chose tool and die making as a career. I, on the other hand, didn't submit my life to Christ until I was in my early thirties, and only then did I really begin to study the Bible. After about two years of serious Bible study, I wanted to be baptized, and it was Steve who baptized me.

Other people thought we were crazy for going at all. "Don't you know *they* (meaning Muslims) want to kill us?" Still others said five years wasn't long enough. "You'll just be getting the language." It was true, but we never felt like we were being called to stay in Mozambique indefinitely. We felt God had a *specific* work for us to do. We just didn't know exactly what that might entail.

My favorite question was, "Are you going there to help people or to share the gospel?" as if the two were mutually exclusive. To that query, I replied a resounding, "Yes, absolutely yes!"

Although some of the comments were hurtful, most were encouraging. Eventually we had to just bend our ear to God and tune out the other voices. Thankfully our family was supportive of our decision. That helped a lot and we would come to know other missionary families who did not have that blessing. Part of counting the cost was counting the sacrifice *they* were making by letting us go.

We began the process of disentangling ourselves from our life in the USA.

Disentanglement was not an easy process even though we had worked hard to become debt-free by that time in our lives. I owned a veterinary practice of fourteen years. It included real estate with a hospital, barn, and two rental apartments, which I needed to sell. We also had a home on acreage with horses and hayfields, dogs and cats. What would we do with all that? In time, God provided a family—from our church, none the less—who wanted to rent our house and agreed to look after the animals and the hayfields. May God bless them.

I closed my practice and put it up for sale so I could work on raising the rest of our support, our travel arrangements, and get the training I needed. I found a wonderful realtor who would later become a faithful supporter of the work in Mozambique to market the veterinary hospital.

We needed several weeks of training in cross-cultural ministry and language acquisition. I also wanted to get some training in human medicine and tropical diseases as well as participatory methods of teaching community health. Steve wanted to get additional training in water wells and pump repair. We needed to raise support and we needed to support ourselves until all this was accomplished. It was a daunting task, and we didn't know how to go about it. It was a time of excitement mixed with anxiety and uncertainty, but God provided and gave us affirmation along the way to help us get through it.

We lived off Steve's salary as he continued to work, getting as much training as he could during his vacation time and also taking time off without pay. We had our sights set on departing for Portugal for language study in August, only six months after our survey trip to Mozambique. As per CVM rules, we had to have at least our first year's start-up costs as well as commitments for eighty percent of our ongoing support raised before we could leave the country. A dear friend and former client committed to paying the entire cost of our cross cultural/language acquisition training. So, in faith, we booked the five-week course for May trusting we'd have adequate support by then. Because Steve had no more time off, he would have to resign at the end of April in order to get the training. We were confident we would make the goal as we were already very close to eighty percent.

But then the goalposts moved in April, just when Steve was about to give notice. The economy had made a dramatic downturn in the previous six months and many churches and supporters of other CVM missionaries were no longer able to fulfill their commitments. The director at CVM was faced with the difficult decision of laying off support staff so they would not have to bring some missionary families home that were inadequately funded. In order to keep new families from being sent out only to have them return for lack of adequate support, they changed the policy to require commitments to meet one hundred percent of ongoing support.

The change put us in a quandary. If Steve quit his job and the rest of the support we needed didn't come through in time, we wouldn't be allowed to go out *and* we would be unemployed. As if that weren't bad enough, we had already promised to rent our home to the other family beginning in July, so we would be *homeless and unemployed*!

On the other hand, if he kept his job, we wouldn't be able to go to the training we had already paid for and the program was booked through the end of the year. So our departure would be delayed by several months during which time we would have no home. We didn't like the thought of being in limbo that long.

I was in North Carolina getting medical training when I got the news about the policy change. It was just two days before Steve was to give notice to his employer. We discussed our options over the phone and prayed. We decided to trust that God would provide and to stick with our plan. He had called us—certainly He would make the way for us to go. Steve turned in his two-week notice the following day. Steve and I had both gotten our first jobs as teenagers and had stayed in the workforce in the decades that followed. So it felt weird for *both* of us to be unemployed, not knowing how we would manage if the rest of our support did not come through before our savings ran out.

We prayed some more, but we didn't have to wait long. The very next day I got an email from CVM saying they had received two more pledges of ongoing support that brought us up from eighty percent to ninety eight percent of what we needed. They said we had the go-ahead to finish our training and leave for Portugal in August. Phew! It may have been only a baby step in faith from God's perspective but leaving a good job in a down economy without the security of another felt like a giant leap for us.

Despite the affirmation of God's provision, we still struggled some days. There was so much to do before we left. We were relieved to have a nice family rent our home, and yet we had many preparations to make on the farm so that it would be easier to manage. Most of this burden fell on Steve's shoulders as it involved things like fence building and laying water lines. He was really feeling the strain one Friday evening as we drove to our favorite Chinese restaurant.

Steve is a disciplined man who thrives on structure and routine. He doesn't like change. It makes him anxious. I am not so disciplined and tend to be overly optimistic that things, like change, will work out somehow. I am fond of telling people that I am an optimist, and he is a pessimist, but Steve corrects me to say he is a *realist*, the implication being that I am not. He may be closer to the truth.

As we were driving along, he was listing all the obstacles to overcome, and I was countering with my rosiest projections of how it would all work out. But despite all my encouragement, or maybe because of it, his anxiety level kept rising. I realized I wasn't helping, so I decided to quit trying and silenced myself.

By the time we reached the restaurant, you could cut the tension with a knife. I came back from filling my plate at the buffet to find Steve attentively listening to an elderly gentleman whom we'd never met; we'll call him "Mr. B." As I neared the table, I heard Mr. B saying with great intensity, "I don't know who you people are or what you are preparing to do, but I'm here to tell you that *you serve a mighty God and He will bring it to pass!*"

We were a little dumbfounded as Mr. B continued. "I didn't even know why I came here this evening. I was supposed to go home and meet my wife, but the Spirit led me to this place. Then I saw you two—and saw the Holy Spirit all over you—and knew *you* were the reason He brought me here tonight!"

Mr. B was a pastor of a local congregation and he shared a little of his story with us. As a young child from a poor family, he suffered from a terminal heart condition and eventually became too weak to stand. The doctors told his family there was nothing more they could do for him and that he would not live much longer. That was when his family took him to a small church where a revival meeting was taking place. Since he was "going to die anyway," they carried him up to have the pastor and others lay hands and pray over him. That was when the young Mr. B was miraculously cured! He jumped to his feet and ran around the church building. He said, "The Lord's Spirit has been strong on me since that day, and I've never quit serving Him."

God is so good! We returned to the house that evening at peace with the assurance that we do indeed serve a mighty God and He will bring *His* plan to pass.

In the book *God Calling*, the author wrote, "Joy is of two kinds. The joy born of love and wonder, and the joy born of love and knowledge, and between the experiences of the two joys lies discipline, disappointment, almost disillusion."[2]

That evening we were still operating in the first joy. Sometimes God gives us a vision on the mountain top, a glimpse of His plan, and an inkling of wonders to unfold. Then, we return to the valley. The hardness of the immediate task before us makes it is easy for us to lose sight of the vision. The mountain visions are great, but we work out our salvation in the valleys where we must walk by faith. It is in those valleys that we discover the joy born of love and knowledge. It is *this* joy that no man can take away.

On our journey we would pass through many valleys of discouragement, but oh how we relished the mountain views. Bringing them to remembrance would help us to recall the mountain vision and encourage us through the valleys. How amazing that the Creator of the universe invites us to participate in the

---

[2] *God Calling,* edited by Russel, A.J., entry for April 17. Barbour Publishing Inc., P.O. Box 719, Urichsville, Ohio 44683. Used with permission.

coming of His Kingdom—the reconciliation of a lost world back into His presence through the blood of His Son, Jesus Christ. What a privilege it is to play a small part in His master plan.

Chapter 7

"The Lord . . . will send his angel with you
and make your journey a success . . ."
—Genesis 24:40, NIV

The Portuguese explorer Vasco de Gama arrived in Mozambique in 1498 and the Portuguese began colonizing the territory in 1505. Mozambique did not gain independence until 1975, so the Portuguese language became the fully entrenched national language after five centuries of colonial rule. For us to survive in that country and deal successfully with government officials, a working knowledge of Portuguese was essential. In the villages of Niassa province, however, most of the men and almost all the women and children speak Chiyao, their heart language. Many cannot speak Portuguese aside from customary greetings. Although we hoped to eventually gain proficiency in Chiyao, we needed to learn Portuguese first. English speakers in that remote province were few and far between and there were no language schools. Therefore, to learn Chiyao from a local language helper, fluency in Portuguese was necessary to communicate with the helper. In other words, we would have to use our second language to learn our third language.

We decided to spend nine months in Portugal engaged in intensive language study, at the advice of our teammates. That was the amount of time they spent in Portugal when they were in their twenties with more pliable brains and much better hearing. I was forty-six and Steve was fifty-four years old. He had significant hearing loss, so we knew we would need at least nine months and probably would have benefitted from a full year. But we also felt a sense of urgency to get to Mozambique, knowing our time was limited, so we applied for nine-month student visas.

Perhaps the powers in Portugal that decide matters like visas did not believe that we could truly be students at our age because, after much delay, they granted us tourist visas instead. They were only good for three months. Even so, in faith, we went forward with our plans hoping that once there we could convince them to let us stay longer. I searched online for apartments near the language school because we wouldn't have a vehicle. It took some time, but I finally secured one within our budget, a challenge as the euro was much stronger than the dollar.

In May 2009, we went to Mission Training International (MTI) in Colorado for five weeks of study in language acquisition and cross-cultural training. We were thankful for that training as it proved to be invaluable in the field. Also, we were blessed to befriend other missionary families and singles we have stayed in contact with through the years. It has been exciting to see how God has worked in their lives just as He has in our own.

When we returned to Texas in June, we had to move out of our home to make room for our renters. We moved into the veterinary hospital, which still had not sold. We camped out in the clinic area, because the apartments were rented. It was the beginning of our nomadic life, but we adjusted fairly well thanks to the memory foam we put on the lumpy sofa that became our bed. Meanwhile, we continued to make final preparations for our departure.

Just two weeks before our departure date, we got a good cash offer on the hospital. I was thrilled because being an out-of-continent landlord was not an idea that I relished. We accepted the offer, and the deal closed in record time according to Donna, our realtor, and everyone at the title company. God is so good, it was one less entanglement. Of course, it also meant moving again, but we were happy to oblige. We packed the rest of our belongings and went on a road trip south to visit my parents in the Texas hill country. Then we traveled north to Oklahoma to spend the last few days with our children and grandchildren. By that time our second granddaughter, Ellie Kate, had been born and it was a joy to spend time with her and Chloe, our first grandchild.

Our departure date, August 9, 2009, finally arrived. Our family took us to the airport where we said our good-byes with tears of sadness mixed with the joy of anticipation. The faith it took for us to get to that point seemed small compared to the faith we needed to press on. I felt a sense of relief when the plane lifted off the runway; we were really on our way and there was no turning back now. I felt at peace knowing we were in God's hands. It was a peace I would take with me from then on. It was a peace that would see me through difficult times and help me to see God's hand in every detail of our lives.

Our overnight flight to London was smooth. We had a five-hour layover at Heathrow. We had made living arrangements over the Internet with a couple in Portugal named Katja and

João. They offered to pick us up at the airport in Lisbon and take us to the apartment they had secured for us. We'd be arriving on the evening of the tenth and were supposed to call them upon our arrival. However, we were unable to get our phone unlocked[3] before we left so we could use it in Portugal. Our plan B, if we were unable to call, was to take a taxi to João's real estate office where he would meet us.

As we waited for our next flight, we were a little apprehensive on how we would manage once we arrived in Lisbon. We had five large suitcases, two backpacks, a computer, and a guitar. I wondered if the taxis in Portugal were small cars or if we would be able to secure an SUV. We also didn't know how far João's office was from Lisbon or how much it was going to cost.

Once we were in the boarding area, I spotted a kind looking lady that I thought might be able to help. I asked her if she was familiar with the Lisbon airport and if they had large taxis available. She said, "Oh yes, I am very familiar with the airport and they do have some larger taxis."

They announced the boarding call and we were separated in the chaos because instead of lining up, everyone just pushed their way forward. Even Steve and I got separated for a short time.

Several minutes later, I was walking down the aisle of the plane looking for our seats. There she was again! The kind lady's seat was right next to mine. We started chatting immediately, and I learned her name was Manuela. She was Portuguese and a native of Macau, a former Portuguese territory off the coast of China. Manuela spoke

---

3   Each country has its own SIM card, which allows you to use it in their country. To get out of our cellular provider's contract, since they did not service Portugal, we had to get a code from them which enabled us to use a SIM card from Portugal.

English perfectly. I later learned that she also spoke Cantonese and Danish in addition to her native Portuguese. She asked where we were going and when I showed her the address, she said it would be very expensive to take a taxi there—maybe a hundred euros! Later, when she saw how much luggage we had, she said it would have taken two taxis.

I had planned to sleep between London and Lisbon because I hadn't slept at all on the previous flight and was exhausted. But Manuela and I continued to visit and we became fast friends. She immediately took it upon herself to help us in our predicament. First, she volunteered her phone, only to discover it was out of power. Then, she looked at the address again and said, "I know this place, it is across the street from my mother's apartment. I tell you what, you can come home with me on the train. It will be much less expensive, and from there we will call João to pick you up."

True to her word, Manuela took us under her wing and guided us out of the Lisbon airport to the bus, which took us to the train, which took us to her home in Pared. Late that night, twenty-four hours after we left Texas, we finally arrived at our new home. I had never seen anyone show such kindness to two total strangers, but it was plain to us all that the Lord had brought us together because we needed each other and would end up being lifelong friends in Christ.

Manuela had been widowed five years earlier when the love of her life, Carlos, died unexpectedly of a massive heart attack. He was only in his fifties and after five years, she still couldn't speak of him without tears mixed with smiles and laughter, still very much in love. Her loss caused her to seek out God and, since Carlos' passing, she had grown ever closer to the Lord. She had been faithful to Him in worship and prayer. More recently, however, she also felt compelled to study the Bible in earnest. She had been raised in the Catholic faith but had never really studied the Bible. In her own words, she just read it occasionally as she would a novel. She had been returning from a conference in Walsingham, England the night we met. The conference was part of a charismatic movement within the Catholic Church. Manuela was fed and inspired to begin studying the Bible seriously but did not know where to begin and had no one to study with. "We can help!" I quickly volunteered.

A few days later, Manuela treated us to a traditional Portuguese seafood supper at her home. We began to meet every Friday evening. Steve and I usually caught the train to Pared and we would have a time of Bible study and prayer with her and her friends. Then she'd cook a wonderful Portuguese or Chinese meal for us. Other times, she would come to our little apartment for tea and study. Sometimes we'd all go to Lisbon, where she would show us historical sights on a "walking tour." After the tour, we would find a nice park to have coffee and study the Word. Another time her friend Lenor invited us to dinner at her beautiful summer home in the mountain town of Sintra where we had a bird's-eye view of both a Portuguese palace and the ruins of an ancient castle of the Moors. Wherever we went with Manuela, it was a sweet time of fellowship.

Katja and João also went out of their way to help us get settled into our new home. They spent literally hours with us to get our Internet and phone service and a local bank account established. They invited us into their home and their lives as well and we met their beautiful daughters Melanie and Louisa. All these people were total strangers before we arrived and it caused me to reflect on how much effort I had made in the past to make newcomers feel welcome. I resolved I would do better—be kinder and show more hospitality to strangers and foreigners.

Chapter 8
Language Learning for Dummies

OUR TIME IN PORTUGAL WAS a time of pruning. We learned how to adapt to city life: small spaces, tight living quarters, and high fences. The culture was very different from America, but not as different as Mozambican culture, so it was a good stepping stone for us. We missed the privacy and beauty of our spacious log home in Texas where we couldn't see any other homes. Our apartment in Portugal was small but full of natural light and was only a short walk to the ocean and the train station. The kitchen floor space only measured about three feet by five feet and Steve was strictly forbidden to enter when I was cooking. I struggled to learn how to cook without the microwave and all the pre-packaged foods we have in America. Manuela gave me lots of tips but we basically survived on soup and salad the entire time with only occasional forays into more adventuresome fare.

Our time in Portugal also proved to be one of the wettest and coldest winters on record and our only source of heat was a small space heater. Manuela once again came to our rescue by lending us an additional space heater and a heavy down comforter we named "the Rock" because it was so thick and heavy. A small washing machine was crammed into that tiny kitchen, but we had no dryer. So we hung our clothes outside to dry on a rack attached to the bedroom window. When the rains set in, however, we had to hang a clothesline crisscrossed above our bed to dry the clothes. It took several days for the heavy clothes to dry, and it made the apartment feel even more cramped.

Soon after we settled into our apartment, we enrolled in an "express" course at Margarida's Language School. Steve was leery of the class from the start because of the term "express." He is very methodical and prefers thorough explanations and detail; he is a linear thinker. At Margarida's, however, the instructors preferred using the "immersion method." That means only Portuguese was spoken in class. The texts were also written exclusively in Portuguese.

Got a question? Get an answer in Portuguese. Still don't understand? Get further explanation in Portuguese. Only if you have steam coming out of your ears, as Steve did once, or break down and cry, which I felt like doing a few times, do you get a few words of English. It is a great method for young pliable brains, especially children. That is the way children learn language after all; they are immersed into the language of their parents. Unfortunately, however, it is much harder to learn language by osmosis as you get older. One should take note that even children do not start speaking intelligibly until they have been "immersed" for about two years.

I had an advantage over Steve in that my hearing was better, and I had studied French and a little Spanish in high school. Although I had forgotten almost all of it, at least I was familiar with the process of language learning and how to conjugate verbs and so on. It was strange to me how, as I strained my brain to remember a Portuguese word, the French word would pop out of my mouth instead. Suddenly all these French words I thought I had forgotten were right on the tip of my tongue—it was very annoying—and yet I could not help but marvel at the way God designed our brains to learn language.

Poor Steve had never studied a foreign language, and the immersion method was not working at all for him. He stuck with it and endured the initial express course, but became very discouraged until Michael, a new friend from church, came to his rescue with an offer to give him private lessons and a textbook that had explanations in English. Michael, a retired math teacher, was British but had lived in Portugal from the time he was seven years old. He and Steve worked well together, and Steve's stress level went down as he began to make progress.

I continued on at Margarida's school and began to enjoy class and the people I met there. But language learning is hard work, and if anyone tells you otherwise, I can assure you they don't know what they are talking about. It is also a humiliating process. Think about it. You arrive in your new country having achieved a certain level of success in life. You feel you are intelligent and skilled in your area of expertise. Then, you are reduced to communicating your thoughts like a two-year-old: "Me thirsty"; "Me want water"; "Me no understand"; and "Speak English?"

It helps to not take yourself too seriously and to be able to laugh at yourself. You might as well because everyone else is laughing at you. I think God has a great sense of humor. He enjoys teaching us the humility we need to serve Him. Maybe that is why He sends us to foreign lands where we are sure to be stripped of our pride and dignity. Thankfully, Steve and I did learn to laugh at ourselves and the quirky process of language acquisition.

Nevertheless, it is not my intention to diminish the necessity of learning another's language. To share the gospel, it is imperative. As the apostle Paul said, "There are many different languages in the world, and every language has meaning. But if I don't understand a language, I will be a foreigner to someone who speaks it, and the one who speaks it will be a foreigner to me" (1 Cor. 14:10–11, NLT).

Studying Portuguese, and later Chiyao, gave me new insight into this passage. Learning the vocabulary is not the most difficult part, nor is learning the word order of the sentences. For me, the most difficult part is learning the *way* things are said. Let me give a few examples.

That fall, when the cold wet weather set in, everyone kept telling me they were "*constipada.*" I thought: *That is a little too much information, thank you!* But after the third or fourth person said this, I realized it probably didn't mean what I thought it meant. So I looked it up and, lo and behold, it meant they had a cold. The condition we know as constipation is portrayed much more poetically in Portuguese as "prison of the belly."

That was a funny one, but others were much more aggravating. Even if you succeeded in choosing the correct word-for-word translation with the proper sentence construction, you may still be met with puzzled looks. For instance, I had looked up the word "walk" and the dictionary gave the Portuguese word "*andar.*" So the first time I tried to use "*andar*" in a sentence, I told Guida, my teacher, "I walk to school" using a word-for-word Portuguese translation. I was pretty happy with myself. It was only the third week of school and I'd conjugated the verb correctly and remembered all the words. I was surprised when she shook her head and said, "No, we don't say that." We say, "*Vou à pé para escola.*" Literally, "I go by foot to school."

You might be wondering when it's appropriate to use the word "*andar.*" You can "*andar*" by plane, "*andar*" by bicycle, or "*andar*" by horse. You can also "*andar*" any process over a long period of time (like learning Portuguese). If you are scratching your head like I did, you are beginning to understand some of the difficulties of language acquisition.

Thankfully, we were prepared for this phenomenon in some of our training and were specifically told not to ask too many "why" questions about language as it gets you nowhere. Languages are what they are and they belong to the people who speak them. The sooner you accept the differences and quit asking "why," the better off you will be and the less annoying you'll be to your teacher.

It is also true, however, that every language is not without its own power of expression. Occasionally you might discover a wonderful idiomatic expression. I discovered my favorite of these just before Christmas. Guida asked me to relate the story of Christmas in Portuguese.

I got stuck when it came time for Mary to give birth to baby Jesus. I didn't know the verb for "to give birth." She said, "dar a luz" —literally, "to give the light." Wow, what a beautiful way to describe the birth of Jesus Christ. Other Scriptures started coming to mind . . .

> "I will also make You a light to the nations that My salvation may reach to the end of the earth" (Isaiah 49:6, AMP).

"In Him was life, and the life was the Light of men. And Light shines on in the darkness, and the darkness did not overpower it" (John 1:4–5, AMP).

I asked Guida if Mary was the only one who "gave the light," thinking it may only refer to Jesus' birth, but she said, "Oh no, we all do it. I did it."

Again, I thought, *What a powerful expression . . .*

There it was—the true Light which, coming into the world, enlightens everyone. But to as many as did receive and welcome Him, He gave the right to become children of God" (John 1:9, 12, AMP).

Through it all, we persevered in our study, enjoying the delights and enduring the difficulties of our new language. Eventually, we gained a working knowledge of Portuguese before leaving the country. We were by no means fluent yet, but we had gained enough proficiency to survive in Mozambique. There we would continue the learning process, eventually gaining fluency despite our personal challenges.

In my morning times of prayer and Bible study, God's Spirit continued to affirm that He was in control of every detail of our lives and our journey. He would bring His purposes to pass.

Chapter 9

"... that they all may be one ... so that the
world may believe that You sent Me."
—*John 17:21, AMP*

IN THE YEARS LEADING UP to our departure for Mozambique, we had been privileged to travel to Uganda, India, El Salvador, Burkina Faso, Rwanda, and finally Portugal. Along the way we met so many of God's family in Christ that I lost count. But I found a strong family resemblance despite the physical differences and the language barriers. It is truly an amazing thing to travel half way around the world and meet up with family who take you in and care for you as one of their own. I get really excited when I consider what God has accomplished and will accomplish through His children. He is up to something big, nothing less than reaching all the nations, tribes, and peoples on earth. His family is not loud; they are humble, serving faithfully, and overcoming evil with good by His power. Before closing the door on our time in Portugal, let me briefly share with you the story of one of His children that we met while there.

Caroline was an English nanny in her midthirties when she gave her life to Christ. Although she was a new believer, she immediately had a strong desire to serve in missions in Africa. She frequently skimmed through missionary journals looking for opportunities to serve, but became disheartened over time to find the requests were always for doctors, nurses, and clergy. She wondered why God had put this strong desire in her heart if she was not qualified to go.

Then, one morning she was sitting in church as a letter from a missionary serving in Mozambique was read out loud to the congregation. The year was 1995 and thirty years of war in Mozambique had finally ended, but the country was devastated. The war left deep scars on an already impoverished nation and had also left thousands upon thousands of children as orphans.

The missionary was working at an orphanage that was home to six hundred of these little ones with only a skeleton crew of men to care for them. She put out a simple plea for help. "We need someone who can wipe children's noses." Caroline perked up immediately, thinking, *I can wipe children's noses; I've been doing that all my life.*

It wasn't long before she was in Mozambique serving at that very orphanage, which was also where she met Michael, a school teacher. They soon married, with a crowd of orphans to witness, and spent the next twelve years serving together in Mozambique.

Caroline and Michael were two of that great family we met in Portugal at the International Christian Church where we worshiped. When Steve was struggling with the immersion method of language learning, it was Michael who gave him private lessons at no charge. Yes, they were family.

We also met many others at that little church who would become friends. Ken and Maria, an American family, were professional musicians who played for the Lisbon orchestra. Vanessa was a student from Belgium with a passion for transformational development. Karen, also an American, was a teacher at the International Christian School. And I can't forget Pastor Carlos and his family. They were Portuguese, but had lived many years in Mozambique and still had a passion for the people of Africa.

I also met new friends at the language school. Wan Sook, a sweet Korean lady, was also learning Portuguese. We became language buddies. Steve and I had many good times with her and her husband. Wan Sook was Buddhist but had a Christ-like, servant heart.

It was fitting, like bookends, that we shared what we thought would be our last night in Portugal with Manuela. She had ushered us into Portugal and insisted that we spend that last night at her house for a time of prayer and fellowship with her, Lenor, and another friend before we left. They prayed with us and over us and promised to pray for us the entire time we would be in Africa. The next morning Manuela drove us to the airport and we said our good-byes. I was surprised at how hard it was to say good-bye to that dear friend and sister in Christ, after knowing her only eight months.

We never did receive those elusive student visas, but by re-newing our tourist visas twice, we were able to extend our stay to eight and a half months. We had booked a flight back to the USA shortly before our visas were to expire for the third and final time. When we arrived at the airport, however, we discovered that a giant cloud of volcanic ash had delayed our return flight, which was routed through London. Thankfully, the airline arranged for us to spend the night in an elegant hotel in Lisbon and rerouted us the following morning on another airline that went directly to Newark, New Jersey. We later learned that had we flown to London as planned, we would have been stranded there for many days, and the airline was not paying for the accommodations. We, on the other hand, arrived safely in Texas only a few hours later than planned, thanks to the direct flight. Furthermore, we did so at no additional cost. Once again, I was reminded that we were in His hands, and He was caring for us.

Chapter 10

"As the Father has sent Me, I also send you."
—John 20:21, AMP

WE LEARNED SO MUCH DURING our time in Portugal. Of course the primary goal was to learn Portuguese; but God had also pruned us quite a bit. He taught us to trust Him while learning to live outside our comfort zone. We also witnessed the unfolding each day of God's plan for our lives. We were constantly amazed at His provision as well as the steady stream of souls that He brought across our path who needed the comfort of our Savior. Much like Elisha's servant (2 Kings 6:16–17), our eyes were opened to the reality of the spiritual battle going on all around us.

We had a few months back in the States to reconnect with family, friends, and our home congregation in east Texas before departing again, this time for our first two-year term[4] in Mozambique. We also used the time to share the vision of bringing the Good News to the Yao through transforming relationships built on servant love with other churches in Texas and

---

[4] Steve and I were committed to five years, our sending agency, however, only wrote up contracts for two to three years at a time, max, knowing many don't manage to finish two to three years in a remote area much less five.

Oklahoma where we had ties. Then, we began final preparations for the move to Mozambique. We were gladdened by the kindness of friends and family who welcomed us into their homes and loaned us a car to use during those months because we had rented our home and sold our vehicles before we left for Portugal. We had also purchased a shipping container and left it on our property, partially packed.

Nomba village did not have electricity, so we purchased solar equipment and carefully re-packed the belongings we thought would be most useful there. We had left most of our furniture in our home to be used by our renters rather than have it destroyed by rats in Mozambique or pay for storing it five years. But we did take our bed and that lumpy sleeper sofa out of the vet clinic and two comfortable chairs, all of which we thought we would leave in Africa when the time came instead of shipping it back to America, which would have been costly. Steve took all his tools, and I took quite a lot of medical equipment and supplies. Then we worked out the logistics of shipping. First, the container would go to Houston, then to a port in northern Mozambique where an agent would get it through customs for us. Finally, it would be transported by a large truck across northern Mozambique on mostly unpaved roads, eventually reaching the village. As it turned out, even though the container began its journey a month before our own departure, it did not arrive until *six months after* we did, due to the terrible road conditions.

There were also things like doctors' appointments—vaccines and malaria prevention—and visa applications that had to be done. I got my continuing education requirement for my veterinary license completed. And Steve squeezed in a short-term mission trip to Honduras with Living Water International. There he got additional training on well drilling. It was a busy time but that was hard for people working a "normal" job with a set forty-hour work week to understand. People asked us if we were having fun "just hanging out." I couldn't blame them; I might have thought the same thing had I not experienced just how much preparation it took for such a move.

I did, however, take some time out to ride my horse. I was heartsick about leaving our pets, especially the horses, for such a long time even though we were leaving them in good hands. So whenever we were in our hometown, I took every opportunity to ride. That was how I ended up in the hospital with a collapsed lung just weeks before our scheduled departure for Africa.

I fell off my horse after a jump. Although the outpouring of love from friends was overwhelming, I did get a few "what were you thinking doing something so dangerous?"

I wondered the same thing . . . for a moment or two. But consider my perspective: I had spent a large portion of my adult life standing directly behind the kicking end of a horse with my entire arm inserted where the sun doesn't shine.[5] Spending time in a totally unnatural position that screams DANGER! makes a person realize that being on the *back* of a horse, where God intended, doesn't seem so dangerous after all.

As it turned out, I spent three long days in the hospital reflecting on my passion for horses. It was Winston Churchill who once said, "There is something about the outside of a horse that is good for the inside of a man." It was a sentiment I could totally

---

[5]   Equine veterinarians use rectal palpation to diagnose various conditions in horses such as pregnancy and colic. It is a dirty job but somebody has to do it!

identify with because being around horses has always refreshed my soul. It was a passion I must have been born with because I didn't grow up with horses. As far back as I can remember, however, "a horse" was my response to every inquiry about what I wanted for every birthday and Christmas. A plastic horse was what I received each time instead. I ended up with a very large collection of them, but God had a plan for that passion of mine.

In recent years many people have said to me "you are so brave—going to live in a third-world country—I could never do that." But I have a confession to make. I am not brave, not one bit. Do you remember that scrawny clumsy kid in gym class who was always the last one picked for the team because she was a liability to whichever team got her? That was me. I was terrified of anything requiring strength, agility, or athleticism because I was such a klutz. I always got hurt whenever I tried such things. I much preferred reading . . . safer, you know. I didn't even learn to ride a bike until I was in the sixth grade because I was afraid of falling and getting hurt. If it had not been for the determination of my friend Margaret, I would probably never have learned, but she just kept insisting. I finally got it, thank goodness! Her efforts to teach me softball didn't go as well. The first time the ball came at me straight from her bat, it hit me square in the nose, which broke (confirming my fear). That was the end of that. Yes, sports were too dangerous; reading was much better.

Thank goodness for horses! Despite my fear of all things painful, God put such a desire in me to be around them that I was willing to risk getting hurt. The same year I learned to ride a bicycle, my parents finally gave in and said I could take some horse-riding lessons. I was in heaven and soon spending as much time as possible at the stables cleaning stalls, hauling water, feeding, grooming, whatever needed to be done in exchange for extra chances to ride. I was shocked to learn that *my* body was capable of making muscles too!

I received an even greater surprise the first time I fell off. The instructor didn't even ask if I was hurt, but instead ordered me to get back on the horse—*immediately*. I did and I survived only to repeat the cycle from time to time. I developed a tenacity and perseverance that served me well later in life. And all the hours I spent just observing horses—how they go, how they communicate, literally everything about them—also paid great dividends when I became an equine veterinarian many years later. People think our patients don't talk to us, but they do. You just have to know the language.

As I lay in my hospital bed thinking, *Was I being stupid?* I realized something. I shudder to think of the fearful person I would be today if God had not put that passion for horses in me. I'd probably be too afraid to pursue anything difficult (like veterinary school) or ever step out of my comfort zone. I definitely would not have gone to Mozambique. But God is so great and yet so tender. He knows each heart so well and just what is needed to bring us along, to grow us but not break us.

It was not bravery or a sense of adventure that caused us to leave everything familiar and begin a new life in Mozambique. So the question remains, how *do* we respond to the call of God and the command of Jesus to go and be His witnesses? The word in Acts 1:8 translated as "witnesses" comes from the Greek word for "martyr." Jesus was saying, in effect, that through the power of the Holy Spirit, we will go be His martyrs, if need be, in order to bring His message to the world. How do we get that kind of faith and place everything at His feet? The truth is that if we wait until we are confident that our faith will never fail, we will never go, and we won't be His witnesses.

We need to know the Scriptures, but all the Bible study in the world will not be enough to grow our faith if we don't act on what we already *know* to be true. "So be careful how you listen; for whoever has [a teachable heart], to him more [understanding] will be given; and whoever does not have [a longing for truth], even what he thinks he has will be taken away from him . . . My mother and My brothers are these who listen to the word of God and do it!" (Luke 8:18, 21, AMP, emphasis added).

The point is you cannot study your way into a relationship with Jesus Christ. We can never get there by our own devices. The only way to get through the fog of doubt and disbelief is through obedience. Obedience in whatever matter the Spirit of God has placed on your heart will lead to more faith and the ability to trust Him enough to obey in the next thing. It is through obedience that we grow in faith.

"Since by your obedience to the Truth through the [Holy] Spirit you have purified your hearts . . ." (1 Pet. 1:22, AMP). It is also through obedience that God works through the Holy Spirit to purify our hearts.

"[Live] as obedient children [of God]; do not be conformed to the evil desires which governed you in your ignorance . . . But like the Holy One who called you, be holy yourselves in all your conduct . . ." (1 Peter 1:14–15).

Obedience to God is not a one-time event that ends with our baptism. It is a continual lifestyle, believing in Christ and living in a way that reflects that belief, and *that* leads to holiness. If our lifestyles do not stand in stark contrast for good in comparison to the way of the world, then what message are we witnessing? We must get down to the bedrock of our faith, and that is Jesus Christ. We must not shrink back in fear but instead be bold, be courageous, and not be ashamed of the Gospel of Jesus Christ. It *really is* Good News. It is the power of God for salvation to *all* people (see Romans 1:16ff).

Yes, the truth was Steve and I committed to go to Mozambique out of obedience, not bravery. Once we obeyed, however, God granted us the courage we needed to follow through, and our faith grew as a consequence of that obedience.

Not long after my accident, Steve also ended up in the hospital when he tore the meniscus in his knee while loading the container. He had arthroscopic surgery that went well and he soon got the okay to travel. Our departure was only delayed a few weeks, and it was a blessing. It allowed us the opportunity to meet our third granddaughter, Lillian Jewel, who was born the week before we flew out.

We said our final good-byes to family and friends. This time the good-byes were even harder, knowing we were going to a dangerous part of the world (at least, that is how we perceived it) and wouldn't have our first furlough for two years. Then we got on the first of four flights and reached Lichinga, the capital of Niassa province, four days later. Upon arrival, we were greeted by our teammates and new family in Christ, who took us to the village of Nomba, located about six miles outside of the city. At last we had made it to that village in northern Mozambique we had set our sights on two years previously. At times it seemed like we hit so many hurdles we would never arrive, but we *had* arrived, in God's perfect timing.

And God's promises are certain. "Everyone who has given up house or brothers or sisters or mother or father or children or property, for My sake and for the Good News, will receive now in return a hundred times as many houses, brothers, sisters, mothers, children, and property—along with persecution. And in the world to come that person will have eternal life" (Mark 10:29–30, NLT).

We trusted His Word and stood on His promise.

Part 2 First Year in Mozambique,
August 2010–July 2011

Chapter 11
Mozambique

FROM THE TIME OF OUR survey trip to Mozambique in March 2009 until the day of our return there in August 2010, I had read everything I could find on the history of Mozambique and the history of the Yao people. I had also read the Quran and as many books as I could about Islam and ministry to Muslim peoples. Yet, I had only scratched the surface. Here are the highlights of what I learned.

Mozambique is located on the southeastern coast of Africa and the history of civilization in this region goes back thousands of years. Bantu-speaking[6] people arrived in the area around the time of Christ. They migrated from the interior of Africa and traveled along the great Zambezi River basin, which cuts through the southern one third of the continent. By the ninth century, Arab traders who sailed the Indian Ocean began trading with the people along the east coast of Africa and a string of prosperous city states were established. Unfortunately, their trade included African exports of both ivory and slaves.

The Arabs also brought their religion, Sunni Islam, which

---

[6] *Bantu* refers to a cluster of related languages spoken by various tribes of central and southern Africa, much as Latin is used to describe the languages derived from that language—namely French, Spanish, Portuguese, and Italian.

was eventually adopted by some of the African tribes including the Yao, the Makua, and the Makonde of Northern Mozambique. Portuguese explorers first visited the area in 1498 and by 1505 had established their own trading posts in direct competition with those established by the Arabs. The slave trade that began with the Arab merchants continued under Portuguese domination and flourished as European plantations were established in North and South America in the 1500s, greatly increasing the demand for slave labor. By the 1820s, Mozambique was deporting up to thirty thousand slaves a year from the port of Quelimane to Brazil and Cuba. Meanwhile, the slave trade of the Arabs continued but the primary destination of their captives was to the Middle East and Asia. It has been estimated that Mozambique lost approximately two million people to slavery.[7, 8]

Prior to the arrival of the Portuguese, the Yao had developed strong ties with the Arabs. In exchange for cloth and firearms, the Yao provided the traders with ivory and slaves captured from other tribes. Firearms gave the Yao a significant advantage over neighboring tribes, with whom they were frequently at war. Consequently, the Yao became a much-feared as well as rich and influential tribe.

In 1885, European powers divided Africa into colonial territories without regard to traditional tribal boundaries. Portugal, Great Britain, and Tanzania each took a share of the traditional homeland of the Yao people between the Rovuma and Lugenda rivers and in the hills surrounding Lake Malawi. The three co-

---

[7] Much of the historical information on Mozambique is used from Joseph Hanlon, *Mozambique: The Revolution Under Fire*, Zed Books Ltd., London.1984, permission requested.

[8] Hanlon, *Mozambique*, 16.

lonial powers laid claim to Yao territory in what would become Mozambique, Malawi, and Tanzania respectively. Consequently, Portuguese, English, and German became official languages of the territories. The Yao, however, maintained a strong cultural identity—for example, continuing to use their own language—that transcended national boundaries.

Like the Arabs before them, the Portuguese also brought with them both their trade and their religion, in this case, Catholicism. Catholicism was adopted primarily by the tribes of the southern and middle sections of Mozambique, while Islam continued to maintain strongholds in the northern provinces and coastal towns. Both the Islam and the Catholicism adopted by (or imposed upon) the various tribes were mixed with the traditional beliefs practiced by the population prior to colonization. Although the Yao were Sunni Muslim, the Islam they embraced was intermingled with witchcraft, spiritism, and ancestral cults. This intermingling of beliefs resulted in a religion referred to as "Folk Islam."

With the increasing dominance of the Portuguese, the status and influence of the Yao began to decline. As pressure increased from Christian influences later in the nineteenth century to stop the slave trade, the Yao grew highly resistant to Christianity, which they viewed as having a negative impact on their own economy.

In 1891, the Portuguese government, having few resources to maintain their claim to the colony, leased the Northern one third of Mozambique out to foreign business interests to maintain control over it. The British Niassa Company received the provinces of Niassa and Cabo Delgado while the Mozambique Company received Manica and Sofala provinces. A third British company, Sena Sugar Estates, established themselves in the central Zambezia province. Meanwhile, the government expected Mozambicans living in the southern provinces to supply cheap migrant labor for the gold mines of neighboring South Africa.

As an incentive for the foreign businesses to operate in Mozambique, Portugal provided them with an abundant supply of cheap labor by the imposition of a yearly head tax placed on every African for the privilege of living in their own land. The value of the head tax was equivalent to the total wages an African man would earn in six months of hard labor. All Africans had to carry documents showing their work and tax records. The head tax, collected by the business from the workers' wages, also ensured revenue for the Portuguese government.

Although slavery was illegal by the twentieth century, forced labor was not much different from slavery. The employer only paid a man enough to keep him alive and pay his tax. The cost of food, clothing, and housing for the entire family was carried by the wife at home who worked the family plots of land. Author Joseph Hanlon describes the living conditions of the company workers in his book *Mozambique* as follows: "Living conditions were so bad that workers became increasingly debilitated. At night, five to eight men slept on the floor of each straw hut with only blankets to cover them. There were few latrines and no running water . . . the men worked twelve-hour shifts and the night shift was locked in . . . [They] had one meal a day and that was mainly flour, which they had to cook themselves, and often ate raw because they were too tired to cook. Furthermore, they received their days ration only if they finished their assigned task." [9]

For the company, on the other hand, the six-month term of

---

[9]   Ibid., 19.

forced labor was ideal. It allowed them to exhaust a man physically and then send him home to his family for six months to recover. The company paid nothing to the cost of supporting him or his family. Many men would die on the long walk home at the end of their contract.[10]

In 1928, the fascist dictator, Antonio Salazar, came to power in Portugal. As if to add to the misery of the Mozambicans, the new government imposed forced cropping on the women in addition to the forced labor required of the men. Authorities required each woman to raise one acre of cotton to support Portugal's textile industry. Women who failed to grow their cotton were beaten and raped. Forced labor and forced cropping of cotton left less land and labor available for the family farms that Africans had traditionally depended on to feed themselves. Decades of monocropping and over-cropping depleted the soil. Several severe famines of the 1940s were linked to forced cotton growing.[11]

By the 1950s, there was growing unrest toward colonial rule across Africa. That was also the case in the Portuguese colonies of Mozambique and Angola where it had been especially brutal. The misery of the Mozambicans had come to a peak. Colonization had thoroughly destroyed the peasant agriculture and small trading that existed before. Peasants were an integral part of the cash economy and were now required to buy necessities like food that forced labor and forced cropping allowed them no time to make or grow. Yet the wages of their labor were insufficient. Hanlon summarized the situation when he wrote, "Mozambique is one of the poorest countries in Africa not because it lacks natural resources,

---

[10] Ibid., 19–20.
[11] Ibid., 20.

or because Portugal left it undeveloped, but rather that Portugal actively underdeveloped it." [12] It was in this context of suffering that the seeds of revolution began to germinate.

In 1961 Mozambicans formed the Marxist resistance party *Frente de Libertação de Moçambique* (FRELIMO) with the goal of liberating Mozambique from colonial rule. The government of Portugal, however, refused to negotiate with them. From their stronghold in Niassa province, FRELIMO soldiers waged a guerilla war against the Portuguese that continued until 1975 when Mozambique finally won independence. Portuguese civilians and military evacuated the country rapidly, sabotaging water wells and important infrastructure and industries on their way out. FRELIMO forces subsequently took control of the country.

At the time of her independence, Mozambique was already one of the poorest countries in the world. To make matters worse, the new nation was almost immediately plunged into a brutal civil war that would continue another two decades. The governments of white minority ruled Rhodesia and apartheid South Africa were fearful of their communist neighbor and of the message sent to their own masses by an independent, African-majority-ruled Mozambique. The two governments began covertly training and arming disaffected loyalists from the revolutionary war. The loyalists became known as *Resistência Nacional Moçambicana* (RENAMO) and subsequently waged war on FRELIMO forces. As confrontations escalated, however, Rhodesia and South Africa were less covert. At times, both countries waged war on Mozambique directly.

A desperate population was caught in the crossfire of both

---

[12]   Ibid., 22.

wars. During the revolution, the Portuguese secret police had brutalized suspected FRELIMO sympathizers. In the rebel strongholds, however, communists persecuted Catholic nuns and priests. In the civil war, both sides targeted anyone with a university education who could be considered a threat to the power structure that prevailed at any given time. Teachers, doctors, nurses, and even traditional healers were massacred. Schools, hospitals, bridges, and roads were bombed and entire villages burned for suspected sympathies with the opposition. The entire country became a minefield that continued to claim lives long after the war finally ended. "Throughout the 1990s and until recently, hundreds of people were injured or killed by the land mines." [13] Only since 2015 has the country declared itself "mine free."

Conditions gradually began to improve, however, after the government renounced Marxism in 1989 and, mercifully, peace talks and economic reforms soon followed. Mozambique adopted a democratic constitution in 1990, and in 1992, the fighting finally ended. Despite the tremendous strides made in the decade following the end of the war, when we arrived in 2010, the statistics were still dismal. Seventy percent of the population lived in extreme poverty. Infant mortality and HIV/AIDS prevalence rates remained some of the highest in the world, while literacy rates and the average life expectancy of forty-one years

---

[13]   Suarsan Raghaven, "Mozambique Was Once Riddled with Tens of Thousands of Land Mines. Now It Has None," *The Washington Post*, September 17, 2015. https://www.washingtonpost.com/news/worldviews/wp/2015/09/17/mozambique-was-once-riddled-with-tens-of-thousands-of-land-mines-now-it-has-none/?noredirect=on&utm_term=.76169cac5cc2

remained near the lowest in the world. [14]

Even today, infrastructure remains a hindrance to progress as only twenty percent of the roads are paved, most of them near the capital of the country, Maputo, located in the southern most province. Tensions between FRELIMO and RENAMO political factions remain high, periodically erupting in armed conflict, forcing the people to live under the threat of another war.

In a poor country, the Yao are among the poorest people groups in the world. Their territory is roughly thirteen hundred miles from Maputo. Attitudes toward the importance of education are gradually changing, but the people maintain a strong cultural identity and fierce independence. They are by and large peasant farmers and traders on the local markets. They continue to be highly suspicious of foreigners and therefore remain highly resistant to the Gospel of Jesus Christ. Their cultural identity is largely wrapped up in Islam; to be Yao is to be Muslim. With reportedly ninety-eight percent Muslim adherents, they were considered "unreached" in 2010. [15]

---

[14] World Fact Book, on-line resource, Country Profile Mozambique, 2008. https://www.cia.gov/library/publications/resources/the-world-factbook/geos/print_mz.html

[15] Joshua Project, on-line resource, People Group profile: Chiyao Muslim Mozambique, author anonymous, 2009. https://joshuaproject.net/people_groups/15988/MZ

Chapter 12
New Beginnings

"Behold, I stand at the door and knock; if anyone hears and listens to and heeds My voice and opens the door, I will come in to him." (Rev. 3:20, AMP).

Our Lord knocks, our Lord patiently waits for our invitation to enter in, to dwell with us and to lead us into all truth.

> "And you will know the Truth, and the Truth will set you free" (John 8:32).

> *Only in the voluntary surrender of our life to Him do we find truth and freedom.*

> "Live as free people . . . but [live at all times] as servants of God" (1 Pet. 2:16).

> *And the rest of life becomes the aspiration of unbroken communion with God.*

Our first month in Nomba was a mix of busyness and serenity—the certainty that we were in God's hands, just where He would have us to be. My first impression was the tangible weight of spiritual bondage, yet not without seeing the hand of God at work as well. The poverty was extreme and generational following centuries of injustice and corruption, but we were warmly welcomed, and I felt strangely at home. I remember waking up that first morning to birdsong. It was a familiar tune, the same song I used to wake up to at my grandparent's home in East Texas. It gave me great peace deep in my soul. For Steve, it was different. His worst night was our first night there. The sense of separation and loss from leaving loved ones and everything familiar was deep and overwhelming, bringing him to tears. I would have times like that also, but they came months later. For the moment, my curiosity of our new home kept me from dwelling on what we had left behind.

Everything was strange to us. Everyday tasks like shopping and driving required a learning curve, because they were not so simple anymore. We drove on the left side the road. Consequently, the driver's side of the truck was on the right side. You had to shift gears with your left hand, but breaking and accelerating were still done with the right foot, clutching with the left. No big deal, right? But when you add to that the chaos on the roads—people on foot or bicycles, motorcycles passing on all sides, big trucks going dangerously fast, dilapidated cars poking along dangerously slow, goats and children darting across the street—it was unnerving. Plus, we didn't know our way around Lichinga, so we had to concentrate on our driving and search for locations at the same time. It worked well for the first few months to make shopping and driving a two-person job. Steve drove and I looked for the place we needed to find. I wanted to learn my way around before taking the wheel.

One of the first places we became familiar with was the Department of Immigration. We came over on a three-month visitor visa and had to immediately apply for a resident visa. The hope was it would be granted before our temporary visa expired. That is how we met Musa, the big man at immigration. He wasn't as bad as some, but he was sure to let you know this was his territory. You best do things his way, or you simply wouldn't get your visa. The application required our teammates to write a letter of invitation in Portuguese on our behalf, which we would then submit to Musa for his approval. After sitting for an hour or two in the waiting room, our turn would come. He would examine the letter and critique it for us, speaking in Portuguese of course. Sometimes it was a substantial critique. Other times it might be a grammatical error or even a matter of style that he disapproved. We would need to rewrite the letter several times, because he never found all the errors in one pass. Each time would require another morning waiting patiently or sometimes not so patiently, at the immigration office. Arguing was out of the question as was going above or around him. This man held the power to determine if we would be allowed to stay in Mozambique or be sent home. At the very least, he was the first in a succession of government bureaucrats who would need to approve us before being granted the visa.

The whole process probably would have gone much smoother had we offered a bribe. Musa would never ask for one. That would be beneath his dignity, not to mention unlawful, but if one was to offer something to gain favor, how could he refuse? Corruption was rampant in Mozambique. We didn't realize at that time just how deeply and thoroughly corruption penetrated every aspect of life there. In our training at MTI, our instructors forewarned us that we needed to search the Scriptures that relate to bribes and determine, before we arrived in the country, how we would deal with such situations when faced with them. That was good advice.

We had done our homework and determined that we would not pay bribes. Bribes only hurt the poor who can't afford to give them and thus don't receive needed services. We didn't want to make matters worse for the poor in Mozambique, not to mention other missionaries who might come after us. So we'd try to outlast Musa. And when the letter finally met his approval (or he got tired of seeing us in his office knowing we were not going to offer a bribe) he would begrudgingly accept the letter and the application. It was a process we would repeat every August when our resident visas expired. The time and effort it took required that we put other ministry efforts on hold for about three weeks each year.

The other office we would have to get past was the Department of Religious Affairs. Again, the local office had all the authority. Even though religious freedom is constitutionally permitted in Mozambique, the provincial office was staffed entirely by Muslims. Through the years, I received many gray hairs because of my encounters at religious affairs. They were not as subtle and dignified as Musa. Sometimes they openly requested bribes. But neither were they as contemptuous. Thankfully, we had teammates to help us learn how to play the game and keep a positive attitude.

We were well provided for those first few months, because the Hamptons left for their furlough time of three months in the USA the day after we arrived in Mozambique. The timing allowed us to live in their house and use their truck while we worked on our visas and settled in a bit. It also gave us a chance to get to know the other family on the team, Drew and Holly Jackson. We had only met them briefly in the States before coming to Mozambique.

Drew helped us get our documents, and Holly showed me around town. There was nothing akin to a supermarket in Lichinga, but there was central market for vegetables and eggs, a store to buy bread, another store to buy chicken, and yet another store that sold a very limited array of toiletries and packaged foods. The toiletries and packaged foods were imported from either Malawi or South Africa and were very expensive. Although central market also sold meat and fish, I could never bring myself to buy it after seeing it sitting out on the tables covered with flies. The smell in that section of the market was nauseating, so I held my breath when passing through. Mouth breathing was too hazardous due to the abundance of flies.

Holly also gave me tips on food preparation and working with a language helper. She introduced me to her language helper, Jacinta, a stocky Yao woman about my age. She was outgoing and good-humored, even though she had lived through the difficult war years. She couldn't speak English or read in any language, but she was fluent in spoken Portuguese and Chiyao. I decided I would ask her to be my language helper, because Holly was fluent in Chiyao as were others Jacinta had helped in the past. I was eager to begin learning the local language, but I would have to wait until we received our resident visas and found a house and vehicle so I could shift my focus to language learning.

During those first few months, we also got reacquainted with the team at Center for Social Justice (CSJ). CSJ was the resource center our teammates began in 2006 with a Mozambican man named Benne and a group of about twelve people he had personally chosen from the village to work there. We had met most of them on our survey trip, but Betty, Benne's little sister, was an addition to the team. Betty had arrived from Malawi about six months prior to our own arrival. Both Benne and Betty had lived in Nomba as children, because it was the home of their father, who was Yao. After the death of their father, they moved to Malawi. Their mother, who was Chewa and Christian, was a native of Malawi and spoke English, as well as Chiyao and Chewa. Likewise, Benne and Betty spoke Chewa, English, Chiyao, and Portuguese. No one else on the team spoke English, all of them spoke Chiyao, and some of them also spoke Portuguese.

Steve and I enjoyed fellowship with Benne and Betty, because we could easily communicate with them. They were two of the only three Christians at CSJ (aside from our American teammates), so we shared a common language as well as a common faith. I grew especially fond of Betty, who was single and in her early twenties. I thought of her as a daughter. She was encouraging and had a compassionate heart for the poor. She was also fun, easy to be around, and quite beautiful. Steve, likewise, came to develop a fatherly relationship with Benne, who was also single. Benne was in his late twenties, and although he lacked maturity in his walk with Christ, he seemed to have a good heart and a good sense of humor like his little sister.

Both Benne and Betty were relatively privileged, by African standards, after they moved to Malawi. They were by no means wealthy, but their older sister had married a Dutch man who was involved with a charity to help children. Through that organization they were able to go to private school and study at university. Benne had studied business administration and even had the opportunity to study in England. Betty had studied banking. We were impressed with their intelligence and ability to speak multiple languages as well as their desire to help others.

Our relationship with our American teammates had an interesting dynamic. Both couples were in their early thirties, approximately the same age as our sons (my stepsons). So while it seemed natural to have a parental attitude, caring for them as we cared for our own children, we also greatly respected their experience as missionaries, specifically as missionaries living in Mozambique and working with the Yao. They were fluent in the language and understood much about the culture having arrived in Mozambique several years before us. Consequently, in that sense, *we* were the children. They had also gone to a Christian University. The men had majored in missions and Bible. Being young, they had a lot of energy, and the work they had put into learning the language and helping the community through CSJ was impressive. On our survey trip, however, I had sensed there was disunity within the team and some bitterness. I hoped that somehow we could help bring peace and forgiveness. That is what I prayed for.

So, on the one hand, we looked up to our teammates and deferred to their experience. On the other hand, we felt we had something to offer them. In addition to our practical skills in our chosen fields, we added maturity, both in our faith walk and in our life experience, to a youthful team. They had gone to the mission field straight out of college. We, however, spent many years in America before becoming missionaries. Those years included long careers in manufacturing and veterinary medicine, business ownership, and parenting, as well as battling for our faith through the trials of life.

Steve and I both had experienced extended times of depression. For Steve, it was during and following his divorce from his first wife after eighteen years of marriage. For me, it was from burn-out caused by my failure to put God first in my life. As a single woman and a solo equine practitioner, I became a workaholic. I had allowed my passion for veterinary medicine and horses to dominate every aspect of my life to the point of shutting out other relationships, most importantly my relationship with the Lord. Thankfully, God brought us both through those times of testing to a stronger faith before He brought us together.

Once our visa application was accepted, there was nothing else we could do but wait for final approval. So we began spending our mornings joining in the work at CSJ learning about how the work was done, their values, and goals. We were both eager to learn from the team and to discover how God was already working through them. The center included a mixed herd of dairy and meat goats, a few Holstein-cross cows, rabbits, and chickens. I hoped that over time I could find ways to improve the productivity of the animals, thus helping the center gain self-sufficiency. Steve planned to use his training in well drilling and pump repair to help in the area of water development. Our overriding passion, however, was to share the Gospel of Jesus Christ through Bible study groups.

We spent our afternoons looking for a used truck in decent condition and a house to rent that was within our budget. We would eventually build a small house in the village on a tract of land the chief gave us. It was a beautiful site on the southern edge of the village, about a mile away from CSJ and our team-mate's homes. Their homes and the resource center were all situated close together with adjoining property boundaries. Until we could build our house, however, we would have to live in Lichinga, because there were no rentals in the village.

It took several weeks, but we finally located a decent house to rent from the Anglican diocese on the North side of Lichinga. Finding a truck proved to be more difficult. We thought we had saved enough money but soon discovered that vehicles were twice as expensive in Mozambique compared to the United States, because of the huge import tariffs. Mozambique had very little manufacturing even before three decades of war. Almost everything but beer and textiles had to be imported from South Africa.

The year we arrived, hardly anyone had vehicles except government officials, so used vehicles were very hard to find. When we did locate a used government vehicle, it was loaded with all the luxuries. It was also out of our budget—even more expensive than a base model new vehicle. As the time for the Hampton's return grew near, we decided we would have to fly south to Maputo where there were more vehicles to choose from, buy a truck, and drive it "home." So we made plans for the journey.

Chapter 13
The Incredible Journey

"For by Him all things were created in heaven and on earth ... all things were created and exist through Him ... and for Him. " —Colossians. 1:16, AMP

WE MADE THE "INCREDIBLE JOURNEY," as we dubbed it, in October, which is at the end of the dry season in Mozambique. We knew we needed to get home before the rains would begin in November, making the dirt roads impassable. We flew to Maputo, a big city that intimidated us. Steve and I prefer the country and generally avoid big cities as much as we can. We didn't know our way around and it was expensive to stay there. Crime and political unrest were common in Maputo. We couldn't wait to find our truck and get out of there. A bright spot was that we got to meet some of our Good News for Africa teammates, the Hulseys, who lived in a town outside of Maputo. They put us up for the night and gave us advice and directions.

We were also inspired by the Hulsey's personal story of faith and courage to obey God. They told us about the time, some years previously, that they were home on furlough. Their teammates in Mozambique experienced a home invasion in the compound where they lived along with the Hulseys. A group of men armed with guns broke into their home with the intent to rob them and ended up killing the father as well. After the tragedy, the rest of the family returned home permanently. The Hulseys had to decide whether to return to Mozambique. They had children living at home. Their instinct was to protect their children and not return, even though they desired to continue the ministry God had given them. After several months, however, it was one of their children who asked, "We are going back, aren't we?"

They put their lives in God's hands and returned to Mozambique. They continued to live there many years, running a Bible College, long after their children were grown and had returned to America.

After leaving the Hulsey's, we purchased our truck, a base model Toyota Hilux. Then we drove it across the border into South Africa to the city of Nelspruit. We stayed for three days while the truck was outfitted for the rough roads of Northern Mozambique. We added a luggage rack, an extra fuel tank, all terrain tires, heavy duty front and rear bumper guards, rock sliders, and an extra set of headlights that would illuminate far into the distance for night driving. When our truck was ready, we began our journey home.

With the side trip to Nelspruit, we ended up putting two thousand African miles on our new truck using nothing but a map and a compass to guide us. The journey definitely stretched our faith. It was a difficult journey, but we encountered tremendous blessings along the way. In route were two beautiful national parks we got to explore. Both parks were amazing, but the differences between them were telling.

We began our journey home from South Africa at the southern end of Kruger Park. In that park we got to see the amazing splendor and variety of God's creatures up close and personal, as they roamed through the park even along the road, unafraid of people after decades of peace and protection in the park. I stopped going to zoos in America a long time ago because seeing the wild animals confined far from their natural habitat always stole my delight in observing them. In Kruger Park, however, it was pure delight to see them in their natural habitat. We saw elephants, giraffes, zebras, hippos, baboons, black and white rhinos, many varieties of antelope, and birds in abundance. We even saw one lion from a distance.

A few days later, we spent the night in Gorongosa Park in central Mozambique. The park was a spectacular game reserve before the war and was referred to as "the place where Noah's ark landed" due to the abundance and variety of even rare species. Thirty years of war, however, took its toll decimating the animal population to nearly zero. The animals and forests had no protection during this time from local poachers trying to survive and from foreign poachers taking advantage of the chaos to have "open season" on endangered species.

In the years immediately preceding our visit to Gorongosa Park, however, an American man named Carr had dedicated his efforts to restoring the park to its former glory. The dense forests were recovering well and were beautiful to behold, unlike Kruger Park, which was somewhat barren because of overgrazing, exacerbated by drought. But the animal populations in Gorongosa were recovering more slowly than their habitat and the animals were terrified of humans. The elephant population that had lived through the war was still traumatized. Efforts to repopulate another park in Mozambique that borders Kruger with elephants from Kruger only resulted in the elephants high tailing it back to South Africa despite the more abundant food sources on the Mozambique side. Apparently there is truth to the claims about the long memory of elephants. Nevertheless, Gorongosa was another example of God's magnificent creation. I prayed that it would soon be restored to its former glory as new generations of animals would be born that had not seen war.

Between the two parks we drove north along the beautiful coast of southern Mozambique, spending the night at Tsene, located on a pristine section of the coast. There, emerald forests gave way to white sandy beaches. The sand was like deep powder forming low dunes that intersected with the indigo waters of the Indian Ocean. Local fishermen went about their business using nets and dugout boats. There were no motor craft and no noise, just the peaceful lapping of the waves onto the shore. It would have been nice to stay a few extra days, but mindful of the impending rains, we decided it best to press on.

Continuing our journey northward, we crossed the massive Zambezi River and then came to the coastal city of Quelimane, an ancient trading post of the Arabs that predated Portuguese colonization. It was from this city that hundreds of thousands of slaves were exported like chattel from Mozambique, representing eighty-five percent of the exports (by value) from that port by the 1820s. [16]

Except for the delicious giant prawns we enjoyed for dinner that night, nothing compelled us to linger in Quelimane. The sad history of the place and the crumbling buildings depressed me.

---

[16] Joseph Hanlon, *Mozambique: The Revolution Under Fire*, p.16, Zed Books Ltd., London.1984.

When leaving the next morning on the only road out, we encountered an out of control brush fire that encompassed and crossed the narrow road, moving rapidly toward Quelimane. We prayed and continued forward speedily, having no other option, except to try to turn around quickly before the fire reached us. Our new truck was "baptized with fire." Thankfully, no harm was done.

The last two days of our journey we were traversing remote territory. Unpaved roads, rough, hilly terrain, only small villages (no rest stops or toilets) made for a difficult journey. We continued northward, gaining elevation, and the broken pavement eventually gave way to a dirt track. At dusk we came to the small village of Gurúe nestled within beautiful hill country covered with bright green tea plantations. We spent the night in a Catholic monastery recommended to us by a Portuguese gentleman named Rudy who we had met in Tsene. He was a beer distributor for one of the major Mozambican brands and knew all the roads and villages in Mozambique. We were thankful for the recommendation because we didn't see any other place we could have stayed.

As a rule, night driving in Mozambique is a bad idea. If you break down in a remote area, you are on your own as far as food, water, accommodations, and repair of your vehicle. Add to that wild animals and bandits, which are also a real threat. There is no roadside assistance to call. Neither can you dial 911.

The next day, we continued north and slightly west across the mountains to the Niassa highlands (also known as the "forgotten province of Niassa") and the place we called home. Our truck was covered in dirt and dust but had done well throughout the journey. We were likewise dusty and weary but were warmly welcomed by the crew at CSJ and thankful to be back.

Chapter 14
The Challenging First Year

AFTER OUR RETURN FROM SOUTH Africa we had a few weeks left to move out of Thomas and Marie's house before their return from furlough. It was during that time when I first discovered that Benne's character wasn't all that we thought it was. Benne had gone with the Hamptons to America in August with the purpose of introducing him to our home congregation. Thomas hoped to build their confidence in the leadership of CSJ and to share the vision he had for community development in Nomba.

Benne stayed in the US a month and during that time he spoke in front of the congregation from the pulpit. He also stayed in people's homes and shared meals, being treated much as a missionary on furlough. He developed many close relationships, so the trip was successful in that aspect. He then returned to Mozambique while the Hamptons stayed in the US for the rest of their furlough time. It was some time after his return—when we were still living in the Hampton's house—that Benne's sister Betty came to me one day with a heavy heart.

One of the groups that CSJ worked with was a group of women without husbands for various reasons including divorce, abandonment, and death. One of the women of that group had just died from AIDS leaving five young children to be cared for by their grandmother who also had AIDS. The youngest child, Elisa, had been born with HIV and was only eight months old when her mother died. The child was still breastfeeding and was now starving. If there was formula available in Lichinga at that time, I was unaware of it. Nobody even mentioned the possibility of acquiring any. But CSJ had a couple of dairy cows that produced milk that was sold for profit to help sustain the organization. Elisa's grandmother, however, was too poor to buy the milk.

I asked Betty if she and Benne had thought of donating some milk for the child, at least until she was weaned. It seemed to me the obvious thing to do to show the love of Christ—certainly the people who had donated the cows would approve. Betty told me she had asked Benne if they could do just that, but Benne had refused. He said it would create jealousy among the other women. That seemed an odd response, because one of the goals of the groups was to teach people to work together, caring for one another.

"Has anyone *asked* the other ladies if they would be upset?" I asked her.

"No," Betty replied, "we haven't talked to them about it, but Benne doesn't want to. Could you please talk to him?"

I agreed and went directly to Benne. He cited the same excuse that Betty mentioned, but I pressed him saying that it was the right thing to do. They should at least go present the idea to the group. To his credit they did go and, not surprisingly, all the ladies wanted to help Elisa instead of watching her starve to death. But then the *true* reason for his reluctance came out. "Who is going to compensate us for the price of the milk?" he asked.

I was stunned by his question because the cows had been donated to CSJ for the purpose of helping the community.

"God has blessed you with these cows and you are unwilling to donate the small amount of milk needed to feed this child for a few months?"

Benne argued that doing so would cut into their profits and set a bad precedent. I argued that it would show the love of Christ—setting a good precedent—and build goodwill in the community both toward CSJ and toward Christianity. He still refused. I was so sad for them to miss the opportunity to glorify God. I was also sad for Jesus—it seemed like I felt His heart break. Most of all, I was sad for precious Elisa and her grandmother. It was doubtful that she would live more than a few months, maybe a year or two at best, before her HIV would result in AIDS and take her life. The thought of letting her starve to death while we had plenty was just too much for me to bear.

Steve and I had been buying a small amount of fresh milk daily from CSJ for our own needs. After my conversation with Benne, I immediately found Cassimo, the young man who delivered the milk to us every day. I asked him to stop bringing the milk to us and take it instead to Elisa's grandmother on our account for as long as they needed it. I didn't care what Benne thought about it because it was the right thing to do. That was the beginning of an unveiling, if you will, of his true character for me. Elisa would go on to die within a few months from her disease, but I took some comfort knowing that she did not suffer the pain of starvation. I remember praying specifically that God would redeem her suffering in some way.

Around that same time period we also began to realize that the team was somewhat dysfunctional. Thomas confessed that communication between him and Drew wasn't good and they frequently disagreed on how CSJ should be run. Instead of working through their disagreements, however, he said that when Drew was on furlough, Thomas did what he wanted with CSJ. Likewise when Thomas was on furlough, Drew did as he pleased. I began to notice how Benne had learned to manipulate both of them by playing them against each other.

I also noticed that whenever Benne did not get his way he would begin to talk about how much more money he could make if he went to work for a certain gold exploration business in town. This veiled threat to leave CSJ usually resulted in rapid capitulation on our teammates' part. Benne had also convinced them to let him handpick the entire crew at CSJ. He was quick to remind any employee who dared to disagree with him, that they owed their livelihood to him.

On our survey trip, it had come out in our conversations with the Hamptons that the two families didn't worship together. It was unclear to us if they were worshiping at all. Thomas said they used to worship with some of the other missionaries in Lichinga until they decided the others were hypocrites who were more interested in strategizing than worship. He seemed bitter even then, but I wasn't sure who the target of his bitterness was.

We had hoped that out of consideration for us as newcomers they would accept our invitation to worship together. Shortly after our arrival in August, however, the Jacksons politely refused our invitation. They said Sunday was their family day and suggested we consider the Anglican Church in Lichinga. Thomas told me he "got enough church" through their work in the village. I wanted to ask, "What about your family?" but held my tongue. Instead, I told him that worship with other believers was very important to us and vital to our spiritual health. Much to my surprise he replied, "Yeah, I can see that since you are new on the field"—as if the need for corporate worship was something we would mature out of over time. It was clear that neither family wanted to worship with us. Both families had shown us hospitality and kindness in other ways, so we tried not to take offense.

Shortly after our arrival, we also learned that both families planned to leave Mozambique in eighteen months. Their focus during that time would be to transfer the management of CSJ into the hands of local leadership. We hoped eighteen months would give us enough time to develop our language and culture skills as well as our relationship with the team at CSJ. Our biggest concern was dealing with government officials so we would not be expelled from the country.

We moved to Lichinga in November and settled into our rental house in the Anglican Diocese compound, also known as Kuchijinji. It was a nice little house with a veranda on the front and a view of Lake Malawi in the distance. The lake was surrounded by low mountains that took on a violet hue with the setting of the sun. When we first moved in at the end of the dry season, we couldn't actually *see* the lake for all the dust, but people kept assuring us it was "right over there." Then the rains began in late November. The dust cleared and the lake appeared as a sliver of silver at the base of the mountains. We thanked God frequently for the beautiful view from our home. It refreshed our souls and reminded us that He was in control of our circumstances.

We were also thankful for our neighbors in Kuchijinji. Bishop Mark was an American, a forester working for the Mennonite Church, when he first arrived in Mozambique, decades previously. But then he met Helen, a British lady and an Anglican. After they married and he completed the appropriate training, he was ordained bishop over Niassa province. He was very down-to-earth, despite his long robes, and we greatly enjoyed his stories of the history of the area.

Helen, likewise, was a gracious host inviting us to spend our first Christmas in Mozambique at a gathering they held in their home for all the area missionaries. Holidays are especially lonely times when living in a foreign culture, so most of the missionaries in the area made an effort to come together to celebrate Christmas. Even though the missionary community in Niassa province included Australians, Brits, Chinese, and South Africans, they also enjoyed celebrating Thanksgiving—a uniquely American holiday. Although the community was small, it was made up of many different denominations as well as nationalities. But denominational differences were never an issue, a fact that really endeared me to them.

There were other neighbors in Kuchijinji who would come and go, but our favorite neighbor was Rebecca. She had already lived in Mozambique several years by the time we moved in and was still going strong when we left. Her house was literally a stone's throw away. She was an American and had been raised in the Presbyterian denomination. She joined the Anglicans after coming to Mozambique to work on her master's thesis in public health. Because Rebecca was single and great company, we frequently invited her to dinner. Whenever we were discouraged, Rebecca had a kind and encouraging word that helped us get through that difficult first year.

A few days after we moved in, a lady named Rosa came to our house asking for work. She was a petite but muscular woman with a mournful expression and a member of the Nyanja tribe. Almost all Nyanja are Christian and more specifically Anglicans, because they owe their very survival as a tribe to the protection of the Anglican Church.

The British established Anglican missionary outposts in Malawi, known at that time as Nyasaland, in the 1860s. Following Dr. David Livingstone's request, Bishop Charles Mackenzie took on the position of being the first missionary bishop in the area. The Nyanja lived in villages along the southern end of Lake Malawi and they were in constant fear of the Yao who worked with the Muslim slave traders to capture members of their tribe to sell. Some say that had it not been for the protection of the British, the Nyanja would surely have come to extinction.

Rosa was a single mother of three sons, only one of which was still living at home. She named her last son "Sofrimento," which means "suffering" in Portuguese. Names denoting extreme hardship and suffering were common in Mozambique. Rosa lived only a short walk from Kuchijinji and was a member of the Anglican Church that met there. I told Rosa she could work part time for us, to do laundry and prepare lunch. Laundry had to be done by hand and cooking was all from scratch, so giving Rosa a job helped both of us—allowing me time to continue my work at CSJ in the mornings and language study in the afternoons.

Steve also spent time at CSJ and on language, but his primary focus was building our home in Nomba. He wanted to be ready to start building as soon as the rains ended in April. He had already completed the design and obtained a building permit, so he began trying to line up a brick layer. Finding good help in Mozambique is never an easy process. Steve went to building sites around town and examined the workmanship. When he found what he liked, he tried to track down the man responsible for the work. He went down several rabbit trails and almost hired the wrong man, who took credit for work he didn't do. In the end, however, he found a man named Chikopa who did the foundation and brickwork on our home under Steve's supervision. Chikopa worked with his uncle, Kaliba, and another man named Frankie.

Our storage container arrived in February. By the time it was released from customs at the port, the rains had begun and the roads were soon impassable across Northern Mozambique. It felt like Christmas when it finally arrived! We were overjoyed to have our cookware, dishes, vet supplies, tools, that lumpy sofa, and most of all our bed! The local mattresses were a piece of foam cut for short people. Consequently, Steve's feet hung off the end of the bed. When we put our king size bed into the little bedroom of our home, it filled the entire room. Rosa only had one word: "Big!"

It was during that first rainy season that I came down with malaria for the first time. I didn't know what hit me. I thought I had a bad case of the flu or food poisoning because I had fever, chills, vomiting, and felt achy all over. Within hours, my head started to throb, and I felt severe pain in my internal organs. I had never had that sensation before. It is hard to describe, but it felt as if my insides were knotted and twisted. Between bouts of nausea and pain, I would pass out in a cold sweat.

Steve told the Talbots that I was sick, and they came over to check on me. They were American missionaries who worked in another district but were temporarily living in Lichinga, not far from Kuchijinji. Bob and Corrine took one look at me and said, "She's got malaria. We will get some medicine and come right back."

My nausea was so severe that keeping the medicine down would have been impossible had I not brought an antiemetic with me. I put it under my tongue and waited fifteen minutes for it to take effect. Then I took my first dose of malaria medicine. About twelve hours later I began to get some relief. I took my second dose and went into a profound sleep for what seemed like a lifetime. I don't remember waking up over the next two days except to take my medicine, drink some water, and go to the bathroom. On the third day, I was able to eat a little and take a shower. I remained very weak for several days, only getting out of bed for a few hours at a time. Gradually my appetite and my strength improved and after a few weeks, I was almost back to normal.

Malaria is caused by a protozoal organism that inhabits the red blood cells of its victim. The body, in turn, attacks its own red blood cells resulting in severe anemia and an engorged spleen. The medicine is effective against the parasite only while it is circulating within the blood stream. The organism can also go "into hiding" in the liver of the host. There the medicine cannot reach the parasite, which is in its dormant state. Consequently, it is possible to have repeat bouts of malaria without further exposure to mosquito bites by a process called recrudescence.

Recrudescence occurs when the dormant parasite "wakes up" and goes back into circulation, starting the cycle over again. There was no effective vaccine available to prevent malaria at that time despite much work to accomplish one. The disease can be prevented by taking such measures as sleeping under a mosquito net, which we did, and using mosquito spray. One can also take a malaria "prophylactic" drug such as chloroquine, doxycycline, Larium, or Malarone. Unfortunately, resistance to chloroquine was already present across Sub-Saharan Africa making the drug ineffective. All the drugs also have moderate to severe side effects including blindness, seizures, kidney failure, and hallucinations, making the long-term use of them difficult for some people to tolerate. I was one of those people. Through our years in Mozambique I tried all the available preventative drugs, but I never tolerated them well. Each time I discontinued the prophy-lactic drug, I would come down with malaria within a few months.

Steve quit taking malaria prevention early on but never came down with the disease. We joked that I was his prevention, be-cause the mosquitos seemed to prefer me whether we were in Texas or Mozambique. Likewise, Thomas had malaria several times, once severely, but Marie never got the disease. Many of our Mozambican friends suffered every rainy season from the disease. It was, undoubtedly, the most common cause of death in our area.

After my first encounter with malaria, I was determined never to be caught unprepared again. I kept medicine with me at all times whether in Mozambique or in the US because of re-crudescence. I ended up getting malaria ten times during our years in Mozambique and have had milder recrudescence cases twice since our return. I imagine that sounds frightening to some—maybe a reason not to go to Africa or be a missionary. But I learned some things through suffering with the disease that I would not have learned any other way; so I have no regrets.

Having lived a privileged and protected life, I could not iden-tify with many of the sufferings of our Mozambican friends. I could, however, identify with the suffering from malaria. The dif-ference was that I had the resources to buy medicine to keep on hand. I would not have to suffer too long, and the disease would not progress to death. When I had the disease, I was able to lie on a comfortable bed instead of a mattress made of sugar sacks sewn together and stuffed with grass. I could ask Rosa to do some extra work until I recovered. She willingly did so even while tenderly caring for me. Rosa also frequently suffered from the disease.

It was through the affliction of malaria that I began to grasp the power of prayer. I usually planned my days in Mozambique quite full and it seemed that I always got sick at just the wrong time. For example, I felt at times that God had put a certain person (who did not have a phone) on my heart, and I felt an urgency to visit them. I frequently found, however, that when I did not have the strength to get out, I would pray for the person, and they would show up at my door the same day. The first time it happened, I naturally thought it a happy coincidence. After it happened several times, however, I realized it was no coincidence; God had done it!

"'Not by might, nor by power, but by My Spirit,' says the LORD of hosts" (Zech. 4:6).

One day, one of the guards at Kuchijinji came to my door and asked me to follow him. He led me to an old cement culvert about fifty yards from our home and showed me two puppies that had been born to one of the semi-feral dogs that lived in the compound. I had resolved not to get a dog—knowing how attached I get to my pets—since we planned to be in Mozambique only five years. A painful parting would be the inevitable result. But there they were in the pouring rain, the last two pups from a litter of eight. He said the others had died. I caved. I took them home and named them "Nando" and "Zito." We certainly didn't need *two* pups, but I could not leave the last one all alone. It was not long, however, before I found a good home for Zito and we were left with Nando, our very own Mozambican mutt.

Nando (pronounced Naandu) grew into a large German shepherd-type dog and was quite a character. His feet and tail were too big for his body. One ear stood up and the other flopped down. He was intelligent, but naughty, and was soon nick-named "Nando Malandro" by the locals, which means "Nando the Scoundrel."

Nando loved a good party. The facilities of Kuchijinji were frequently rented out to wedding parties, sometimes with drinking and always with good food and loud music. When a party was going on, Nando would invariably cause some kind of stir. Once he grabbed a sack of beer from one of the guests and ran off. Another time, he caught a live chicken and brought it unharmed to the kitchen, as if making a request for dinner to the cook. Despite his size and guard-dog looks, he was pretty harmless and was actually stolen twice. Each time, however, he chewed his captor's rope in two and came back home. I tried not to get attached to him, but he had such a personality that it was hard not to love him. He even won Steve over and became his hiking buddy after we moved back to the village.

We gradually settled into a rhythm of life that first year despite what seemed to be a constant state of flux. I developed relationships with the rest of the team at CSJ, most of whom were good people. Some were easier to get to know than others depending on their openness and proficiency in Portuguese. I enjoyed working with Cassimo, who seemed to catch on to things quickly. I requested that I work with him specifically to train him in animal husbandry. That idea didn't go over well with Benne for some reason. Instead I was given Xandra and another man named Cassimo (we called him Big Cassimo) to train. Xandra was the shepherd who cared for the goats and cows. Big Cassimo was over the rabbits, until he was fired for stealing chickens. Xandra was rough around the edges. He was nice enough but uneducated and difficult to understand. He was also set in his ways, but he did know each of the animals well and seemed to care about them. It took some time for me to win him over, but gradually he came to respect my ability and began to take my advice. Likewise I learned to respect his honesty and knowledge of his herd.

Of all the members at CSJ, there was one lady that I loved right from the start. Her name was Miséria, which means "misery." She was the cook at the center and a sweet and humble soul who kept her eyes cast down most of the time. I remember the day she shared her story. We were all talking about the importance of education. Some of the men, like Xandra, said it was better to work and make money than to waste time going to school.

Miséria felt differently. She told us she never had the opportunity to go to school. When she was a young child, her father was murdered and her mother subsequently went insane. Miséria was sent off to live with relatives and, as frequently happens in such cases, was treated like a servant instead of a family member. She said, "I would give anything to learn how to read! I work hard now so that all my children will have the opportunity to go to school."

My heart was touched and I told her that I would like to help her learn to read some day. We would have to wait, however, until my language was good enough for us to communicate easily. Marie gave me a disapproving look and said I shouldn't make promises. I don't blame her for being protective over Miséria. Marie didn't know me well, and perhaps I had spoken too soon.

That spring Benne married Anna, a sweet young lady from Malawi. He had been courting her since his return from the USA. Steve and I drove to Malawi for the wedding and we took Betty and Elias, a friend of Benne's, with us. The road to Malawi was not paved and just driving there before the end of rainy season was an adventure. By the time we arrived the truck was covered in mud. We met Benne and Anna's families and had a good time celebrating with them at the wedding.

The rains tapered off in April and Steve began construction on our home with Chikopa and his crew. Chikopa lived in town and didn't have any means of transportation. So every morning Steve would leave out at six a.m. to pick up the men and load the truck with supplies before continuing on to the village. Steve developed a good relationship with the men, and we continued to be friends with them long after the work was over. Kaliba would be killed in an accident within two years. He was riding to work when the car he was in collided with a public transport van. These vans were known locally as *chappas*. *Chappas* were always overloaded with people and baggage and were driven at breakneck speed even on treacherous roads. They were frequently the cause of serious accidents, with mass injuries and deaths.

Frankie had the hardest job of all—mixing cement by hand in a wheelbarrow and carrying the bricks to the others—but he never complained. Frankie was a young man, lean and muscular from all his labor, but he had a mild manner and soft speech that belied his muscular frame. He was Nyanja and carried his New Testament with him. One day he asked us to pray for his sick child. He had already taken the child to the hospital, but to no avail. Steve and I prayed with him and I gave him some medicinal plants to treat the child. The child was soon healed completely. Frankie came to visit us several months after the house was completed, walking several miles from town out to the village. At the end of the visit, he asked us to pray for him to find a better job so he could support his family. Once again, we prayed together and then he went home. We wouldn't see Frankie again for almost two years.

We hired a woman from Nomba named Guida to cook lunch at the building site every day. She cooked Xima (the cornmeal mush staple) and beans almost every day for lunch over an open fire. Guida was a plump and sturdily built Yao woman. Unlike most Yao women in the village, she was fluent in Portuguese and easy to communicate with. She had a big smile and quick laugh and was the single mother of six young children. She brought the youngest, Nandinho, with her every day. He stayed in a sling on her back while she worked. Nandinho absolutely adored his "Uncle Steve."

Also in April, Drew introduced me to a man named Abamia who showed up at CSJ wanting to help the orphans in the village. I was already planning to start some kind of ministry for the most at-risk children in the village. I thought I should wait at least a year so that I could learn the language better before becoming overloaded with ministry. When Abamia showed up, however, I considered the possibility that God had opened the door and did not want me to wait any longer. So I talked to Abamia about how we might work together.

After meeting with Abamia, I met with the management at CSJ—Benne, Betty (his younger sister), and Aly (a childhood friend of Benne's). I asked if they were interested in pursuing a ministry with children. If I could raise the financial resources for school supplies and school uniforms, maybe they could help with some of the teaching programs that they were already doing in the village on sanitation. I also hoped to enlist help to teach the children Bible stories. At their suggestion, I presented the idea to the entire crew at lunch one day. Everyone agreed it would be a good thing to do, so I asked them to prepare a lesson on hygiene in the form of a play.

Abamia knew the kids, but he was a Muslim with no knowledge of the Bible. Benne, Betty, Anna (Benne's wife), and Aly were the only Christians at CSJ, but they were too busy to teach the kids. We had recently met another young man from the neighboring village of Ntoto named Julio. He had come to Christ a few years earlier. He had also suffered great persecution because of his faith. As is frequently the case in Muslim culture, the persecution was at the hands of his father, who was grooming Julio to be a leader in the mosque.

Julio had already committed much of the Quran to memory and was praying in the mosque one day when he heard a voice say, "Don't do that." He had been kneeling, eyes closed, with his face to the mat. He sat up and looked around. Seeing no one, he began to pray again. A second time, however, the command came, "Don't do that." Again, he looked and saw no one. More hesitant this time, he began to pray once more. A third time he heard the voice, "Don't do that!"

Julio did not know what to think about the voice, but he left the mosque and never returned. Sometime later he became very ill and was hospitalized. A group of Christians came and prayed over him and he recovered soon afterward. They shared the Good News about Jesus with Julio, and he gave his life to Christ. When his father found out, he became incensed and threw Julio out of the home.

Julio worked with YWAM (Youth with a Mission) and was eager to help me by teaching the kids. Our plan was to meet with the kids on Saturday mornings to teach them Bible stories and praise songs intermingled with lessons on hygiene, sanitation, and disease prevention. Abamia would organize a soccer program for them. I would raise funds so that each child enrolled would receive school supplies and a school uniform. Although primary school is free in Mozambique, the cost of school supplies and a uniform is enough to prevent a child from going to school.

We went to the chief of Nomba and discussed our plans to work together and what the program would entail. We asked for his blessing and help in identifying the neediest kids in the village. He gave us encouragement and offered a tract of land for the program where we could garden produce to help the children. I worked out a budget, and we were able to offer enrollment to sixty children. The enrollment filled rapidly. We soon had a waiting list of another thirty kids who attended the meetings but couldn't receive the school supplies for lack of funding.

My hope was to eventually develop the program into a holistic ministry after the model of Compassion International. I wanted to move forward carefully, however, until I got to know Abamia and Julio better.

Chapter 15
Expectations

AT THE TEAM MEETING SOON after our arrival in 2010, our American teammates had explained to us that they wanted to put, in their words, a "black face" on CSJ. They instructed us to help at the center as advisors but not to join them any longer when they did work in the village. As they prepared for their departure, they were in the process of transitioning to local leadership. They wanted the community to see CSJ as Mozambicans helping Mozambicans, not Americans helping Mozambicans. Going forward, their work and ours would be behind the scenes.

That was also the reason that our teammates had secured a building site for our home on the other side of the village from where their homes and CSJ were located. The physical separation between our home and the center would be a tangible sign of CSJ's independence from foreign influence once our teammates left.

We supported the goal of local autonomy for CSJ. Additionally, we felt that it freed us to pursue other lines of ministry, independent of CSJ. On our survey trip in 2009, I had been adamant about wanting to work with disadvantaged children. I expressed that desire again at the 2010 meeting. Thomas, Drew, and Benne were all present and none of them discouraged me. On the contrary, Drew had encouraged me that, in the Yao culture, helping orphans would be considered a worthy endeavor and a good way to get involved in the community.

The problem was, that while our American teammates wanted us to be *less* involved at CSJ, that expectation was not communicated well to our Mozambican teammates (with the exception of Benne). We were soon to learn that *they* expected we would be involved with the center at the same level Thomas and Drew had been during the initiation and start-up phases of the project.

The orphan program proved to be popular. Julio did a wonderful job of teaching the children Bible stories. He encouraged them to recite the stories themselves, building their self-confidence. The kids loved learning to pray and sing praise songs while dancing. We also had a big celebration for them on June first, the International Day of the Child. It was a holiday in Mozambique and the closest thing these kids had to a birthday celebration.

Abamia organized some women to prepare lunch for the kids. We began very early that morning with several live chickens to process. Meat of any kind was a rarity for these children. The women also prepared rice, beans, bananas, and salad. The kids arrived around noon, each with their own plate (some came with platters!). After washing their hands, they filed in and sat on large mats we had placed on the grass. We sang songs together while the women made final preparations. Then the kids went through the food line filling their plates with as much food as they could pile on. Each child got a Fanta to drink and cookies for dessert.

The chief and secretary of the village came and ate with us as our honored guests. After the meal, we all went to the primary school where the crew at CSJ performed a drama on sanitation. The kids loved it! After the drama, Abamia organized soccer games for the boys. The girls jumped rope and played games. It was a wonderful and exhausting day. I came down with a bad case of malaria shortly thereafter.

We continued to meet every Saturday with the kids through the summer. I had hoped that the crew at CSJ would continue to help with the health and hygiene lessons. But after nudging the leadership several times unsuccessfully for their input, I determined they were not interested in the ministry. Or perhaps they already had too much on their plates. So I taught the hygiene lessons with Julio translating my Portuguese to Chiyao for the kids. Additionally, we provided each child with a mosquito net, toothbrush, and toothpaste in addition to their school supplies and uniform. It was humbling to see the joy these basic items gave the children. The best part of the program, however, was showering them with love and telling them how much they were loved by God. Many of the kids seemed to blossom right before our eyes.

In August 2011, shortly after our one-year anniversary in Mozambique, I met with Benne, his sister Betty, and his friend Aly at their request. Together they made up the management team at CSJ with Benne at the head. It quickly became apparent that they were not happy with me and had already met with each other prior to this meeting. Benne began by complaining about the orphan program. He said that the program was making him "look bad" in the village. I was confused by his claim; how could helping the kids reflect poorly on him?

Then Betty and Aly chimed in saying that all I cared about were the kids. I gently reminded them that I was continuing to work at CSJ as before and was always available when they needed me. In fact, despite the added demands of the children's program,

I still worked at CSJ three days a week and came out whenever they called for an emergency with the herd. I had missed many language lessons while going to treat goats or cows on my days off.

Finally, Betty claimed that I had not said anything about a children's program before I came. She demanded, "So why did you say one thing and do another?"

Flummoxed, I looked straight at Benne and asked him why he had not told the others that I had indeed kept my word and done *exactly* what I said I would do. He quickly looked away and tried to change the subject. He would not admit to them that he knew my plans all along.

Drew was out of the country, so I discussed the matter with Thomas later that day. I expressed my concern about Benne's dishonesty. It bothered me that he had refused to admit that he knew I planned to work with children and let the others think that I had not kept my word. Thomas could have easily rectified the situation by vouching for me, but he seemed reluctant to say anything that might offend Benne. He even made excuses for Benne's behavior.

I was very hurt that our teammates had not stood up for me. My character had been attacked. I had higher expectations of our American teammates than they had lived up to. I thought they would want us to have good relationships with our Mozambican teammates. I felt betrayed. Likewise, Betty and Aly felt betrayed by me. They had expectations of me and felt I had been dishonest with them. Right in the middle of it all was Benne, who was caught playing both sides once again. I realized that Thomas and Drew's loyalty to Benne was strong. They had invested a lot in him and seemed to think that the project depended on him. I wondered when they had quit relying on God.

I licked my wounds and went on trying to do my best in that situation. I focused on 1 Corinthians 13 in my quiet times. I realized that part of loving well is not taking offense and not insisting on vindicating myself. A bond of trust had been broken, however, and so things would never be quite the same.

Steve sympathized with me, but he was more removed from the situation. He was putting all his time into building our home and no longer had time to work at CSJ. He hoped to get the roof on before the rains began and then he could work on the interior during the rainy season.

From that time forward, I continued the children's program without the help of CSJ. Despite the difficulties, God used the children's ministry to open many doors in the village, and He would soon open even more doors in another way.

Part III: Second Year in Mozambique,
August 2011–September 2012

Chapter 16
An Open Door

"Then the angel showed me a river of the
water of life . . . On either side of the river was
the tree of life, bearing twelve kinds of fruit . .
. and the leaves of the tree were for the healing
of the nations" —Revelation 22:1–2, AMP

I MET TERESA EARLY INTO our second year in Mozambique. She was a single mother of four children, and she also cared for her blind grandmother. Teresa provided for them all by farming her *machamba*, a field, usually several kilometers from town, used to grow corn and beans. The poor had to farm land farther out in order to get land that was both fertile and inexpensive. Teresa's *machamba* was forty kilometers from her home in the village of Lumbe Dois, so I knew she was very poor.

One day a storm came up while Teresa was working outside and she was struck by lightning. The current entered the back of both her legs, just under her knees, and exited out the soles of her feet. All the tissue was burned off the bottom of her feet, leaving them looking like raw hamburger. She was unable to stand. Her chest hurt and her heartbeat was rapid and irregular. She was in great pain. Worst of all, she carried the pain of believing she was cursed by God.

The family had no means of transport, but her brother managed to pay for a ride to the hospital in Lichinga. When they arrived, however, the hospital staff told Teresa they could do nothing for her and sent her away. That frequently happens to the poor when they need health care in Mozambique. Like many of the other systems there, the socialized health care system was corrupt to the core. In theory, it was inexpensive and available to all. The reality was the government paid the doctors very low salaries, so the doctors often refused patients who could not pay a bribe. The doctors were poorly trained—usually in Russia or Cuba. I don't know if they refused Teresa for lack of money, or if they truly did not know what to do for her. They sent her away just the same.

Lumbe Dois was about four miles from where we were building our home in Nomba. Her brother had heard about us. He came and asked us to please help his sister. I was not licensed to practice human medicine, and it was illegal for me to do so. I had purposefully been avoiding treating people medically out of fear the government would cancel our visas and send us home if they found out. When I heard Teresa's story, however, I made an exception. She had nowhere else to turn. I gathered some supplies and drove with her brother to her home.

When we arrived, Teresa was sitting outside of her hut on an empty burlap sack placed on the ground. She was crying and looked so forlorn. I examined her feet and listened to her rapid, irregular heartbeat with my stethoscope. I told her I was not a medical doctor, but I would do my best to help her.

I explained that even though I was not qualified to help her,

God could heal her. I assured her that God loved her, in spite of what had happened. I asked her if I could pray for her in the name of my Savior, Jesus Christ, the Son of God. I would ask God for healing for her and to give me wisdom on how to treat her. "Do you believe that Jesus can heal you, Teresa?" I asked.

Much to my surprise, she responded, "Yes. I do believe."

I have to confess, I felt overwhelmed by her condition and had doubts myself. I had never treated a victim of lightning strike, not even a horse, because they don't survive. Typically the owner just discovers the herd of dead horses under a tree.

I didn't know where to begin, so I prayed for us both. I asked Teresa to pray with me, but she said she did not know how to speak Arabic. The Yao are taught that God only hears Arabic, a belief that makes the imams very powerful because they sell prayers. "You can pray in Chiyao, your own language," I told her.

"God hears Chiyao?" she asked.

"Oh yes. God created all the languages, and He hears them all."

After we prayed, I listened to her heart again, and the rate and rhythm were normal. I breathed a sigh of relief—God was working. I made up my mind at that moment that I would treat Teresa using plant medicine. I had been reading the book *Natural Medicine in the Tropics*, published by a group named Anamed. I wanted to see if the plants truly worked. If so, it would be wonderful to train people in their uses. Then they wouldn't have to rely on a corrupt medical system or a broken supply chain of western medicine. Instead, they could get what they needed from the bush or their garden. I did give Teresa Tylenol for her pain. Other than that, I only used plant medicine to treat her. Teresa would be my test case.

I taught her and her family how to prepare saline at home. I showed them how to lavage her wounds with saline. I added papaya latex to the saline to remove the necrotic tissue. Then I showed them how to prepare aloe ferox (a cousin to aloe vera, found locally in the bush) and apply the pulp to her burns. I then covered the burns with paper towels and moistened the paper with more saline. After a few minutes, the paper towel would dry and adhere to the wound forming an inexpensive bandage. I tried to keep the treatments as simple and inexpensive as possible so it would be accessible to the very poor.

I treated Teresa every day at her home until the wounds began to heal. Then, after a few weeks, I came only every other day and let her and her family do the treatments on the alternate days. Teresa healed beautifully over the course of about two months. Soon she was walking again. But the new skin was fragile and would easily tear. She did not have shoes so I gave her a pair of my well-padded running shoes. She tried them on and a huge smile spread across her face—she couldn't believe how comfortable they were.

Not long after she was healed, Teresa walked the four miles to our house to tell me good-bye. She would be leaving early the next morning to go live at her *machamba* in a makeshift hut during planting season. She would take her youngest children with her and leave the older ones behind, so they could stay in school and tend to her grandmother. She would return in a few months to check on her family and get some supplies. I knew she had nothing, so I gathered some supplies from my kitchen—soap, salt, cooking oil, and rice—to send with her for the journey. We prayed and gave thanks to God for the miraculous healing He had done for His child. I prayed for His protection and provision for her and her family and that He would bless the work of her hands. I walked with her to the property line, kissed her on each cheek, and wished her a good journey.

I did not see Teresa again for several months. Then one day she showed up at our house with her eldest daughter, Regina, and a huge sack of beans from her *machamba*. She wanted to thank me for helping her through the most difficult time of her life. It was a struggle for me to receive her gift with grace. The beans she was giving me could be the difference between going hungry and having enough later in the year when her food stores would run low. Every fiber of my being wanted to refuse her gift and tell her to keep it for her family. But instead, I swallowed hard and received her lavish gift with as much grace as I could muster. It was a valuable lesson for me and the beginning of a friendship. The relationship could deepen now because the giving went both ways. Had I refused her gift, I would have denied her the blessing of giving and also put up a barrier. The barrier would say, in effect, "I am greater than you." By receiving her gift, it said, instead, "We are equals and can have a real friendship now."

I asked Teresa if she would like to learn more about the God who had healed her. I had not asked her before because I did not want her to think that her answer would affect my desire to help her. Now that she was healed and providing again for her family, the time was right to invite her to study the Bible. She was eager to learn more, so I began going by her home once a week. Her family and some neighbors would gather round to listen as I played the Proclaimer, an audio version of the New Testament, in Chiyao. We went through the book of Mathew one chapter a week—playing a chapter, discussing it, then playing it a second time. My language skills in Chiyao were not very good at that point, and Teresa's skills in Portuguese were very limited. Discussion was difficult, but it was a start.

Once the word got out about Teresa's healing, more opportunities to help people with the plant medicine would follow in the years to come. God opened many doors for us through that ministry. And, to my knowledge, nobody ever reported it to the government.

I developed a set of guidelines while helping Teresa that I would use in future cases. For my own protection, I would always encourage people to go to the hospital first. If they were either turned away or were not helped by the care they received, then I would treat them. I would insist that I train a family member as well as the patient while treating them so they would know how to use the plants for future problems. I would always pray first and ask for healing in the name of Jesus. When they returned to show me how well they had healed, I would encourage them to pray with me again and give thanks to God. Finally, I would encourage them to learn more about the God who healed them.

Chapter 17
Village Life

STEVE MADE STEADY PROGRESS ON our house and by the next spring we were able to move in. It was wonderful to be living in the village again. We had enjoyed living at Kuchijinji, but it was much easier to build relationships with our friends in Nomba by actually living there.

Living in the village, however, did cause some hardships for us. We still did not have water on our property. The hand-dug well we began only had a few feet of water before we hit a granite slab. We used the dirty water for watering but not much else. We would have to get a borehole drilled. The geography required a rig equipped with air and hammer tooling to get through the granite. It would be expensive and we didn't have sufficient funds at that time. We managed by hauling water from the well at CSJ, about a mile away. Three mornings a week, Guida and I would take six jerricans (five gallons each) to CSJ and pump water. Then we would load them into the pickup, drive home, and carry them into the house. Every ounce of water we used for drinking, cooking, and cleaning was obtained this way. It is amazing how such a situation helps one learn to conserve water!

Steve and I soon perfected the "art" of taking bucket baths using only 2.5 gallons each. Of course, I needed more water on the days I washed my hair. Then, I managed with only five gallons, even though my hair had grown quite long. There was also an "art" to doing dishes. I filled up one tub with soapy water and another tub with rinse water. We wasted nothing and used our gray water for watering the medicinal garden or mopping the floors. We also saved a lot of water by using a composting toilet instead of a flush toilet. After living this way for an extended period, I still struggle when people leave water running when they are not using it.

I don't think I could have survived without Guida. She took Rosa's place in part-time house help after the move, since Rosa lived so far away and did not have transportation. Guida lived only a half mile away and, to help us conserve water, she took our laundry home and did it there. She had a good, hand-dug well at her house.

We also lacked kitchen cabinets and electricity, but we did have a small gas stove. We borrowed a large table, which had a lower shelf, from another missionary family. We set it in the kitchen, and I used it in lieu of a counter to prepare our meals. I kept the dishes in the plastic tubs we had packed them in for shipping. Without refrigeration, I had to go to the market at least every other day. Our dog Nando got all our leftovers.

Everything felt cramped and unorganized. It took a long time to prepare meals, but I got by. Since Steve already had the house wired, we would hook up to the generator at dusk as I finished preparing the meal. We would start our bath water heating while we ate dinner and then quickly take our baths immediately following dinner. The goal was not to have to run the generator more than two hours a day. To run it longer would damage it, not to mention the cost of fuel. After bathing, the generator was turned off, and we would switch to headlights and candles—it was reminiscent of being on a much-extended camping trip.

When we moved in, the rainy season was almost over. Steve's first priority was to get the solar panels set up on the roof during the dry season so he wouldn't have to worry about getting struck by lightning. Running water and kitchen cabinets could wait. Setting up the solar panels was no small task. He had to build metal brackets strong enough to hold the panels securely on the roof in case of 100 mile-per-hour winds. The brackets also had to hold the panels at the optimum angle to the sun to get as much exposure as possible. The brackets had to secure the panels from thieves as well. Solar panels were a high target item for thieves. We brought a nice system in our container because you could not buy them in Mozambique.

By the time he had finished the brackets and installed the solar panels, we had grown so accustomed to not having electricity I would forget to turn on the lights at dusk. Steve would come in and ask me why I was preparing dinner in the dark. It was nice to enjoy dinner and bath time without being in such a rush. Likewise, having a refrigerator and freezer again was pure joy! Less time spent shopping was more time for language study and ministry, not to mention getting to know our new neighbors.

Our neighbors were friendly and curious. We were the first westerners to live on that side of the village. The children would get so excited when we drove by, they would line the road shouting, *"Arungu, arungu!"* which means "White person, white person!" I learned how to tell them in Chiyao "My name is not 'White Person.' My name is 'Julia.' My husband's name is 'Steveni.'" They would giggle and then nod in understanding.

Soon the chants changed to "Julia, Julia, Steveni, Steveni!"[17] When a new kid showed up and mistakenly shouted *"Arungu!"* he would get a jab from the others saying, "Her name is not 'White Person,' her name is 'Julia' and her husband is named 'Steveni.'"

The Yao have a very relational culture, and we wanted our neighbors to feel welcome to come visit us. So we chose not to put a wall around our property. We also had our own selfish reasons for doing this. We had a beautiful view of the mountains from our back veranda, and we didn't want to block our view. Steve felt we would be more secure without the wall, because our neighbors could see if someone who shouldn't be there was at our home. It turned out that Steve was right!

We hired two men who lived close to us to be our guards. Samuel worked Monday through Thursday nights, and Emilio worked Friday through Sunday nights. They were brothers and both lived nearby. They brought their machetes each night. We also supplied them with flashlights and whistles. We met with our neighbors and asked for their help in providing for our security. We told them if a gang of thieves were to show up, our guards would "blow the whistle." We asked them to come to our aid if they ever heard the whistle. Back then, the local police didn't have cars. So if you needed the police, you had to drive into Lichinga and get them. Obviously, that wasn't a good option in the case of a home invasion. Our neighbors agreed to help us and did indeed come to our aid more than once.

---

17   The Yao tend to put a vowel on the end of names, usually "i." So *Steveni* was the natural way they pronounced *Steve*. *Julia* is the Portuguese version of Julie, so they were already familiar with pronouncing my name.

In retrospect, asking our neighbors for help also caused them to take ownership of us in a way. We quickly became part of the community even though we were foreigners. To that end, we tried to get out of our American individualistic way of thinking and adopt a more African-tribal mentality. One example is how we thought of our truck. We were the only people on our side of the village with a vehicle. We wanted to share this blessing with our neighbors. So when our guards tapped on the window during the night to tell us a woman in labor was waiting outside, we gave her and her family members a ride to the local hospital.

Likewise, when a member of our community died, we traveled with a group of men to get the body from the morgue. Not coincidentally, the morgue was located adjacent to the hospital. We would then transport the men and the body of the deceased to the cemetery.[18] Using our truck as both the village ambulance and hearse was just a small way we could make our neighbors' lives a little easier.

We joined forces with some other missionary families in the Lichinga district to negotiate a good price for a borehole. All together there were eight boreholes needed throughout the district, and we were able to get a driller from South Africa to come up at a reasonable price. By that time, we had raised sufficient funds for our borehole, but we had to wait a few more months for some of the others to raise their funds. In the meantime, Guida and I kept

---

[18] The dead are not buried in caskets, they are wrapped in a cloth. The body is transported on a type of pallet carried by the men, with a hollow tube made of basket material into which the body is inserted. The pallet is owned by the mosque and can be used by the members of the mosque. One of the barriers to the gospel in the Yao culture is fear that they would not be buried properly or remembered respectfully after death.

hauling water, and Steve built shelves for a pantry and kitchen cabinets. Once we had electricity and an organized kitchen, it felt more like home and less like camping, even though we still had to haul water.

The dry season lasted from May to October. By August, conditions were very dry and windy. It reminded me of West Texas, but in Texas, when conditions were like that, a burn ban would go into effect. In Mozambique, however, it was time to start burning. Our neighbors were preparing their fields for planting and the easiest way to do this was to burn off the brush. So they set fires in the valley downhill from the village and our home.

One morning, I was working on a report when Steve told me he had to go into Lichinga to get some supplies. He told me to keep an eye on a large fire down in the valley in case the winds were to shift and bring it our way. I finished my report and went to the backyard and saw a huge fire about two hundred yards down the hill, moving rapidly our way. The winds were strong and the tall, dry grass provided plenty of tinder. I went into the house and called Steve's phone only to hear it ringing nearby—he had left it on the table.

Our house was at the southern edge of the village. It was the only thing standing between the bush and our neighbors' houses, all of which had thatched roofs. The village was deserted; everyone was away working in their fields. There was no one to call for help. I tried to stay calm as I got two five-gallon buckets and filled them with water from the hand-dug well. There wasn't much water left. I set the buckets at the southern edge of our property and quickly returned to get some burlap sacks out of our container. Using the sacks soaked in water to beat out the fire would make the water go further.

By the time I got the sacks and ran back to the buckets, the fire had already reached our property line and had surrounded the buckets making it impossible for me to reach them. The fire was now less than thirty yards from the house. I ran back to the well and the only container I could find was a watering can that held about three gallons of water. I quickly filled the can, stuck one of the sacks in it, and ran back to the edge of the fire. I prayed for God to help me as I beat out the fire, making a path to the buckets.

I reached the buckets and went back to the front line of the fire. As I continued to beat out the fire, a peace came over me. As unbelievable as it seems, I was calm as I worked steadily, beating out the fire with my sacks. It even surprised me how calm I was. I remember thinking, *I should be frantic right now. I wonder if something is wrong with me that I'm not afraid.*

I managed to keep pace with the fire, but I couldn't get ahead of it. Then, just as suddenly as they began, the winds died down and shifted to the east. Steve drove up and we worked together to finish putting out the fire. Thankfully, it was no longer heading toward our home but to a ravine east of our property. The result was that we had a good firebreak (burned off area) all around our property after that except for the northern edge, which connected with the village. So if a new fire were to come up the hillside both our home and the rest of the village would be protected.

Before that day, I had wondered why our neighbors hoed out every patch of grass around their huts. It made it so dusty during the dry season. I thought *Why don't they leave some grass around their houses to keep the dust down and make it look nicer?*

Now I understood it was to protect their homes from brush fires. It also helped protect them from snake encounters—we had plenty of those as well. Later that day, I sent an email to my family to tell them about the fire and our recent snake encounters. My sister replied, "Your life is too much like *Little House on the Prairie!*" I had to laugh. That series of children's books about frontier life in America written by Laura Ingalls Wilder was my favorite when I was a child.

We had many adventures living in the village that made good fodder for prayer letters. One night we even had a lion show up in our yard. But the most rewarding part of living there was breaking down the barriers by building relationships. We grew to truly love our neighbors and of all our neighbors, one woman named Lukia, and her children, especially touched my heart.

Chapter 18
Lukia

LUKIA AND HER FAMILY WERE our nearest neighbors. Their property boundary was just to the northwest of ours. Her husband was Emilio, our weekend guard. They had three beautiful children: a ten-year-old son named Bwana, an eight-year-old daughter named Judit, and a four-year-old daughter named Aida. Both Lukia and Emilio were small in stature and their children, likewise, appeared much younger than they actually were. Bwana and Judit had big soft brown eyes like their father. Little Aida, however, had dark sparkling eyes like her mother.

Lukia came to visit with her children soon after we moved in. She brought me some produce from her garden. I invited them in the house and made some tea. Lukia had never been to school, but she spoke Portuguese well, and I had no trouble understanding her. She was outgoing and had a great smile that showed a gap between her front teeth. After we chatted a while, she told me she was a hard worker and asked if I would hire her to clear off the brush from our land.

I had no doubt she was, indeed, a hard worker. Although she was petite, she was also very muscular. She lamented that she could not manage to get fat because she had to work all the time and did not get a lot to eat. I told her that although I was certain she was a good worker, I would like her to just be my friend. I told her I wanted to have at least one friend who did not want to work for us. I asked her if she could be that friend. She agreed, and in the coming years, we grew close. She called me *dada*, the Yao word for *sister* and she called Steve *cunhado*, which is Portuguese for *brother-in-law*.

I loved her children and sometimes they would come over without their mom if she was away. They would frequently show up when I was in the garden and help me weed or plant. It was nice to have children who were not afraid of us. I also visited Lukia in her home and went with her to her *machamba*. She shared many things with me about her life. She kept a tidy house and yard, her children were sweet and respectful, and she and Emilio seemed to have a good marriage. I saw a lot of what was good in the Yao culture by being near that family.

Lukia was especially proud to bring me *otobwa*, a thick drink made from a fermented grain the Yao called "*mapira*." Making the drink was a five-day process and it was seasonal. She made it when the *Unyago* ceremonies were taking place. *Unyago* was the initiation celebration for children passing into adulthood. She said, "We in the village don't have beer or Fanta, we celebrate with *otobwa*. Do you like it?"

"Oh yes, it is delicious. Thank you for sharing it with us. Steve will be so happy!"

Each year she would bring us a half gallon. I'd have a glass with her and the kids—they loved it! Steve and I weren't so keen on it. It was thick like a milkshake, a little gritty, and tasted like slightly fermented sorghum. I knew Lukia worked hard to make it, however, so I tried to drink it all. Steve tried it once and then refused it after that, but not in front of her.

I gave Lukia a ride to the hospital when it was time for her to deliver her fourth child. She said she would rather have the child at home, but the state mandated that children should be born in a local hospital or health post. Doctors were only at the main hospital. The health posts were staffed by nurses or midwives. To encourage mothers to comply, they offered free vaccines and identity documents. If a child was born at home, however, the family would have to pay for the identity documents. From our work in the orphan program, I had learned that many children in the village did not have the identity documents they needed to attend school.

Because Lukia was not a new mother, she only had to go to the closest health post about three miles from our home instead of to the main hospital in Lichinga. When we got to the health post, it was around midnight and was pitch black. I knocked on the door and two midwives opened it but did not turn on the lights. I told them I had a friend in labor who needed to be admitted.

One of them said, "Well, I hope you brought candles because we don't have electricity, and we are out of candles."

Lukia's mother disappeared into the darkness to buy candles somewhere. I had no idea where one could get candles at that hour but she reappeared about thirty minutes later with candles. I had reservations about leaving Lukia but the ladies told me to go home. I told her I would come by in the morning to give her a ride home if she was ready.

The next morning I went by the health post on my way home from market. Much to my surprise, the nurse told me Lukia had already left. I went to her home and she was there with her new son. The other children were gathered around, smiling at their new brother.

"Lukia, why didn't you wait for me to come get you?"

"*Dada,* I hate hospitals. I couldn't wait to get out of there, so I left early in the morning and walked home. What are you going to name my son?" she asked as she placed him in my arms.

I was honored that she let me name him. "Judah will be his name."

Chapter 19

"My Word . . . shall not return to
Me empty . . ." —Isaiah 55:11, NIV

MEANWHILE, THE SAME MONTH WE moved into the village,
our teammates, the Hampton and Jackson families, moved back
to the United States permanently. Before they left, they transferred their houses and the ownership of CSJ and its assets to
the local leadership. They set up the center as a co-op of the
workers managed by Benne with help from his sister, Betty, and
his friend, Aly. Benne's wife, Anna, also helped Betty in the office with the bookkeeping.

Thomas and Drew had asked us to be part of a board of directors that would include themselves (in absentee), Benne, Anna,
Aly, Betty, and Betty's fiancée, as well as three others who worked
at CSJ. Steve and I would only have one vote for the two of us,
but the others would each have an individual vote. Also serving
would be two other outside board members from the area who
were not Mozambican.

In order to receive favored tax status, it was necessary to have
a majority of Mozambicans on the board. We immediately saw
red flags in the way it was set up, however, and I voiced our concerns. I recommended that Benne should *report* to the board, not

be *on* the board. Additionally, we were concerned that the number of Benne's family members and friends on the board would make it ripe for corruption. Drew dismissed our concerns, saying he wanted them to have the ability to "steer themselves." That was the end of the discussion. We could take it or leave it.

It was tempting to simply decline to be a part of something we felt would not continue to function long with Christian values. Even though they had been raised in Christian homes, the leadership at CSJ still lacked much in maturity and development of Christian character. One bright spot, however, was that our teammates had recently convinced Benne to hire Jon, the evangelist from Chenganani, to work with the community groups and he would also be a board member.

Jon was a former Muslim who had come to Christ during the war years. His family had fled to Malawi and was living in a refugee camp when he met a missionary who shared the Gospel of Jesus Christ with him. When he returned to Mozambique, Jon was the sole believer in his village. He preached boldly to the Muslim communities along Lake Malawi despite persecution. Maybe because of the persecution he had endured, Jon was a mature Christian and would be a good influence on the others. Even though we strongly disapproved of the way the board was set up, we agreed to serve on it for a year with the hope that we could mentor the CSJ leadership through the transition.

Soon after our teammates' departure, we asked Benne if we could start holding a Bible study at CSJ on Friday's at lunchtime. We always ate lunch with the crew on Fridays, and sometimes people shared stories and riddles and so on. But we were eager to study the Word of God with people. It was the reason we had come. Benne took a vote and everyone agreed that it would be good to begin a study. We asked Jon to help us, and he was eager to do so. We began in the book of John. We would listen to one chapter on the Proclaimer each week and then discuss it.

Jon was great at helping people to understand the Scriptures. He probably didn't need our help so much, but sometimes he would relay a question to us that he wasn't sure how to answer. Steve would then show Jon where the answer to the question was located in the Bible, chapter and verse. Jon would then read the Scripture in Portuguese, translate to Chiyao, and sometimes give further explanation as needed. I think it helped that we always turned to the Bible to answer the questions instead of just answering them ourselves. It gave authority to the response that our own words would have lacked. People remarked that they appreciated that we did not just give our opinions but showed them the verses. It was Steve's in-depth knowledge of the Bible that allowed us to do that.

We chose the Gospel of John because the Spirit led us there in prayer. Only later did we come to a fuller realization of just how appropriate John's gospel was in a Muslim culture. Muslims know about Jesus as a historic figure and a prophet. But they do not know Him as the Son of God, equal with God. Jesus as God is a radical idea to a Muslim and a blasphemous idea as well. More than any other gospel, John focuses on the divinity of Jesus Christ. I believe that more than any other gospel, John forces a Muslim to a faith crisis.

We were later told by some experienced missionaries to the Yao, living in another district, that John was too confrontational because it "forced them to make a decision." They said it is better to study Luke first and focus on the teachings of Jesus. We had great respect for the missionary who said this but I had to bite my tongue. *Isn't that the whole point?* I thought. *Doesn't everyone have to come to a faith crisis when they make a decision to follow Jesus?*

A few months after we began the Bible study, Betty called me one day. She told me about a young woman in the village who had been badly burned and needed my help. Lucia was a seventeen-year-old mother. She had been in a hut where gasoline was being sold in small containers for motorcycles. It was nighttime and candles were lit. The fumes ignited and caught Lucia's clothes on fire. She was able to quickly get Ana, her infant daughter, off her back, and others put out the fire on the child. But Lucia continued to burn, and they could not stop the fire for a long time. They had no water available so they were trying to smother the fire with corn flour.

When I entered the small, dark hut, Lucia was lying on her stomach, on a mattress on the dirt floor. The mattress was made from old sugar sacks sewn together and stuffed with grass. Lucia had third-degree burns on her entire backside. From her neck to her ankles the skin had been completely burned off except for a narrow strip across the small of her back. Almost half of her body had been burned. Only her head, hands, chest, and feet were spared. I had never seen such terrible injuries before on a human or animal. Ana had second-degree burns on her buttocks and legs. I knew she would heal, but I had doubts about Lucia. Teresa's wounds from being struck by lightning paled in comparison.

I was not equipped or prepared to treat Lucia. She had so many things going against her. The skin is an organ, not just a covering. God designed it magnificently to protect us from dehydration. The most immediate concern I had for Lucia was that she would die of dehydration.

The skin also protects us from all the bacteria in our environment. The second concern I had for Lucia was that she would die of overwhelming sepsis. If she had been in the United States, she would have been put in intensive care with intravenous fluids and antibiotics. Her vitals, electrolyte balance, and hydration status would be constantly monitored by trained professionals. She would be given a morphine drip to control the excruciating pain. Lucia, however, was in a mud hut with a grass roof and a dirt floor. I had none of those things to help her. The family feared the hospital and refused to take her there, certain she would die. I couldn't blame them. By that time I knew of many, with less severe injuries than Lucia, who had died there.

A less immediate concern was her spiritual condition. Lucia believed she was cursed by God. She was in overwhelming pain. Did she have the will to live? Finally, I worried about her long-term future. If she managed to survive, would she be an invalid? Would her body be so scarred and bent that she would be unable to farm? In Mozambique, social systems for invalids were practically nonexistent outside of the family. Would she survive this only to starve to death later? I assessed her condition and knew that Lucia would only survive if God chose to perform a miracle.

Part of me was afraid to get involved, but they begged me to help. I warned Betty that this would take a long-term commitment. If I were to begin treatment of Lucia, I would need a lot of help, daily, for many months. She promised to help me. I tried to talk to Lucia but she was in such pain that she was despondent. Everyone was waiting. I prayed a silent prayer and felt God's peace about going forward. I asked everyone to pray together, and we all did except for Lucia who could not.

Lucia's treatments took over four excruciating hours a day. It did not take long for Betty to grow tired of it, and she quit coming to help. Anna came only once. I asked Miséria to help me. She came faithfully, meeting me each morning. Lucia's mother-in-law, who we called *Anganga* (Grandmother), also helped every day. Because Miséria was the cook for CSJ, sometimes lunch was up to an hour late because she was helping me. Benne began to complain. Dismayed at the hardness of his heart, I suggested Betty and Anna help prepare lunch.

Miséria was wonderful help. She learned quickly and never failed in compassion. We would pray together with *Anganga* over Lucia each morning before we began treatments. Miséria's prayers were always passionate and straight from the heart. She prayed with the simplicity of a child coming to her father—confidant that He was listening.

After we prayed, we would begin. Once again, all I had for Lucia's pain was Tylenol. I would have *Anganga* give her morning dose about an hour before our arrival, hoping it would be in maximum effect during treatment. It took all three of us to hold Lucia up long enough to let her relieve herself into a can before we changed her bandages. Then we would soak her bandages with warm saline and remove them as gently as possible. It was painful and we had to work slowly and carefully so as not to disturb the new skin cells. We also stopped frequently to let Lucia rest.

Then we would clean her wounds with the saline/papaya latex mix. Next we would apply the aloe vera pulp and the new bandages (paper towels) moistened with more saline. After the bandages were well adhered, I would do physical therapy, taking her limbs through their full range of motion several times.

The physical therapy was the worst part. Lucia would scream for me to stop and it felt like I was killing her. I charged *Anganga* to moisten the bandages every eight hours and also to repeat the physical therapy. She did a good job with the bandages, medications, and general care of Lucia, but she couldn't bring herself to do the physical therapy. I couldn't blame her. I knew how important it was but could barely make myself do it.

Amazingly, Lucia survived those first few critical weeks. I began to be hopeful, but I was still very concerned about her spiritual and emotional well-being. Even though her body was responding well to the treatments, she remained despondent, feeling cursed and unable to pray.

I decided to pay Teresa a visit. I told Teresa about Lucia and asked her to come tell Lucia how God had healed her. Teresa agreed immediately and was waiting at my house the next morning. I noticed the shock on Teresa's face when she first laid eyes on Lucia, but she quickly covered it with a warm smile and began to tell Lucia her story. Lucia listened intently but said nothing. Teresa prayed with us and then stayed for the entire four hours while we worked. She held Lucia's hand and caressed her head, praying all the while for Jesus to heal her.

Something changed in Lucia that day. The next day I was greeted with a big smile instead of tears. It was six weeks since the accident and the first time I had ever seen Lucia smile. She had a beautiful smile and it seemed to light up the room. From that day forward, she began to pray with us—thanking Jesus and pleading for Him to heal her. She also began to take charge of her recovery and did her best to bear up to the pain of the physical therapy.

Meanwhile, I read everything I could find about treatment of major burns. The references all stated that skin grafts were required if the burned area was larger than ten centimeters in diameter. Lucia's wounds were many, many times that. I knew at some point the wound healing would stall out and the new skin would quit coming in. I would somehow have to convince Lucia to let me take skin grafts from the precious little skin she had left and transfer it to the burned area. I hated the thought of cutting on her, so I put it off even though she now had a healthy wound bed that would nourish the graft. Amazingly, as I delayed, the new skin continued to come. It wasn't scar tissue, it was skin. Even her normal skin pigmentation began to come back.

We had been treating Lucia over four months and her wounds were about seventy-five percent healed when I heard about a new missionary family living in Lichinga. The wife, Kath, was a physical therapist. I was thrilled and called her. I told her about Lucia, showed her some photos, and asked her to come with me to make some recommendations. It turned out that Kath was not only a physical therapist, but she had worked in one of the largest burn units in Australia. Rehabilitating burn patients was her specialty.

Having seen the "before" photos, Kath was astounded at how well Lucia was healing. By that time Lucia was walking, with a limp, and could go to the latrine by herself. Kath showed Lucia several exercises she could do to improve her mobility. It was a big relief for me to have her input and encouragement.

After almost five months of treating Lucia, I became very worn down. My immune system was weak. I broke out in purulent sores and came down with malaria again. I desperately needed a break. By that time, we had also trained another woman, Maria, to do the treatments. Miséria and I did the treatments three days a week, and Maria and *Anganga* did the alternate days. I decided Lucia was stable enough for me and Steve to take a long weekend and visit Malawi. I received good medical care there and was feeling better by the time we returned.

The next morning after we returned home, I went to *Anganga's* house to see how Lucia was doing. Miséria and *Anganga* were in tears as they told me what happened in my absence. Lucia's mother lived in a distant village near the lake. She had arranged a car and the family took Lucia and Ana by force back to her mother's village. The mother claimed that the people in Nomba had put a curse on her daughter. She wanted to take Lucia back and offer sacrifices to their dead ancestors in the graveyard. She put curses on *Anganga's* family as they were leaving. They said Lucia was crying and didn't want to leave.

I was distraught. Lucia had been doing so well. She was healing both physically and spiritually, but she was still fragile. The unhealed portions of her wounds could easily take a turn for the worse, and she would no longer have the spiritual support we were giving her. Even worse, I knew the mother would anger God by worshiping the spirits of the dead. We didn't know what to do. So we sat down together and prayed for God to protect Lucia and bring her back to us.

Weeks went by. Miséria and I visited *Anganga* periodically and prayed with her. Lucia's husband had gone to plead with his in-laws to let Lucia come home. I sent emails and a prayer letter to the States asking for prayers for Lucia's safe return. Then one day Lucia came back under her mother's supervision. She said she begged her mother to let her come back so she could at least thank me for helping her. Her mother said they would only stay one day.

I was so relieved to see that Lucia was still healing. The wounds had stopped healing with skin, however, and were filling in with scar tissue from not being treated properly. It would cause her to have less mobility than she would have had if she had stayed. But at least she was alive and well. And Lucia had been doing her exercises, which would help counteract the mobility issues.

I talked to her mother with Miséria and *Anganga*. I told her that no one had put a curse on her daughter. On the contrary, we loved her and had been caring for her and praying for her. I also told her that God was healing Lucia, but God would not tolerate her worshiping other gods. I told Lucia that she must give thanks to God alone. She must not participate in any ceremonies for the dead. Lucia assured me she knew it was Jesus who saved her. The mother softened a bit and said that Lucia could stay a week.

We hoped that by the end of the week the mother might allow Lucia to come back permanently, but that didn't happen. We said good-bye with tears and prayed with Lucia once more. I handed her a necklace a friend had given me. It was a fish carved of wood with a cross in the center. I told her the significance of the cross and the sign of the fish to the early Christians. I also told her a special friend had carved it and given it to me, so I could not give it away. I was only letting her keep it to remember us and Jesus until she could return. It was my way of saying "you have to come back to us." I think she understood.

In the meantime, the Friday Bible studies at CSJ continued to go well. Benne joined us less frequently, saying he was too busy, but most of the others seemed to look forward it. Increasingly,

Miséria showed signs of being greatly affected by the Word. I think that the combination of hearing about Jesus' miracles and then participating in what He did for Lucia opened her heart to Him. One day after the discussion, she said, "I've already decided I want to follow Jesus. What do I do now?"

Steve showed Jon, the Bible study leader, the verse from Romans 10:9 and the passages in Acts (2:37ff, 16:30–33) that describe how new believers responded to the Good News. Jon read the passages out loud. Everyone was pensive that day as we closed in prayer.

A few days later, Miséria showed up at our door, her face beaming. She said, "I've been praying to Jesus and He has come into my heart. I have already quit going to mosque. I am only waiting to be baptized."

I was almost afraid to grasp her words; it was too good to be true. She was ready to follow Jesus! "But my eldest brother is out of town on a job until next week," she continued. "I want to wait until he returns to be baptized. He is going to be so proud of me!"

My heart sank. I knew a spiritual battle for her soul was raging. Her brother was going to be angry. We prayed a lot that week. Jon counseled Miséria and two young men, Cascão and Ramos, about becoming a Christian. Cascão and Ramos were not part of the regular crew at CSJ but had been working there as day laborers and had been coming to the study. Jon spoke plainly to all three about the persecution they would endure.

Miséria's brother returned and was furious when he found out she wanted to leave Islam. Her husband was also enraged. They got the religious leaders from the mosque and the neighbors together and the mob threatened to burn her house down with her in it. After three days without eating or sleeping, Miséria was back at our house. She was no longer radiant. The smile was gone. Her face was tight and drawn. Her eyes were cast down. She said she couldn't be baptized, she was afraid for her life.

I hugged her and said, "God knows your heart, Miséria. He has secret believers all over the world who fear for their lives."

We were about to go on furlough, so I gave her our Proclaimer. I encouraged her to wait until things calmed down, then to listen to it whenever she felt it was safe to do so. I admonished her to keep praying to Jesus, and He would give her the courage she needed to follow Him. We prayed together and wept together just as we had done for Lucia.

The following Sunday, Cascão and Ramos were baptized. Miséria and most of the crew at CSJ came to witness. Benne, Anna, Betty, and Aly, however, did not come. It seemed strange that the Muslims all came, but the Christian leadership chose not to come. Steve and Jon read the story of the Ethiopian eunuch and then talked about the significance of baptism using the Scriptures. Then Jon baptized them in the lake. We were told that crocodiles lived in the lake, but that it was "okay" because the crocodiles usually stayed at the other end of the lake. I couldn't help but wonder if I would have been baptized under those circumstances: Would I have followed Jesus into crocodile-infested waters?

We rejoiced with singing afterward, but Miséria's face betrayed her sorrow.

Women returning from a morning of hard work in the bush.

The view from our back porch during rainy season.

Julio teaching the children.

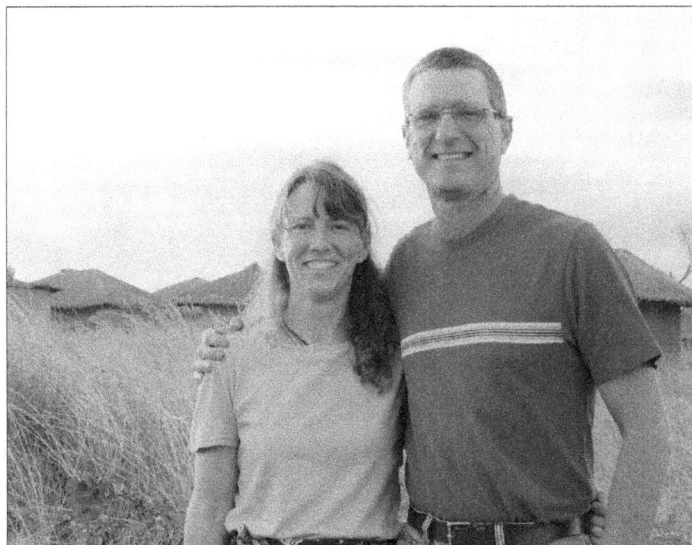

The view of the village from our front yard.

Teresa and her children after she was completely healed.

Lukia and her children on the day
Judah was born (Judit not pictured).

Shortly before she was kidnapped, Lucia was
healing well and had the light of Christ.

Assainabo's family members were the only
Christians in the village of Ntoto.

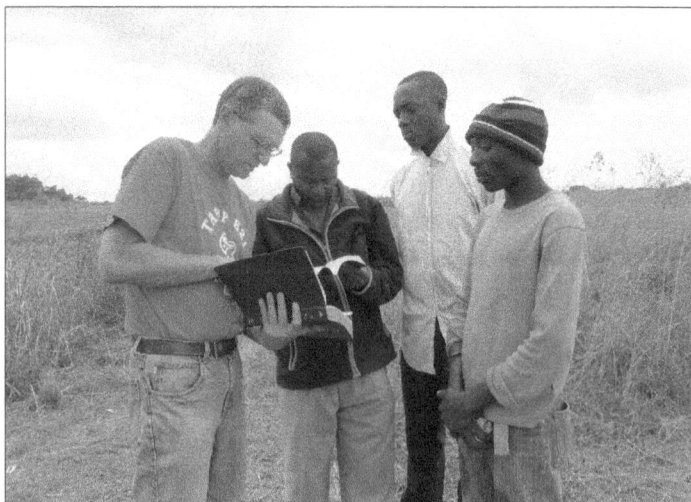

The first to be baptized from Nomba: Steve and Jon
prepare Ramos and Cascão with the Word.

Jon baptizing Miséria in the crocodile infested waters.

Julie and Alegria (formerly known as Miséria).

A year after she was kidnapped, Lucia returned and
gave her testimony to the children.

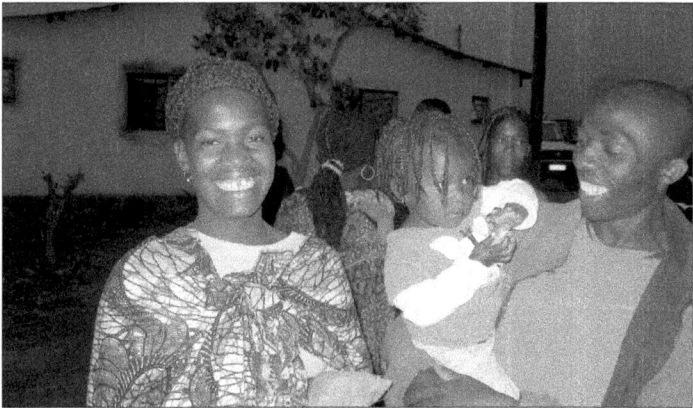

Cascão and Merina on graduation day
from Disciple Training School.

In 2013, the tiny Chengenani church was instrumental in planting the Nomba church. Carolina and Jon—middle row far left. James (their eldest son) and Telma—back row far right

Eighteen months after his own baptism, Cascão baptized Nelito and Paulina.

In a move that surprised us, Nelito carried Paulina out of the water.

Nomba Church in 2014 left to right: Assainabo, Miseria, Julio, Eugenia, Paulo, Steve, Mariamo, George, me with Esperança, Timóteo, Cascão. (Not pictured: Merina, Guida, Rosa, Nelito and Paulina)

The windmill tower Steve built at the Van Stelton dairy farm.

Part IV: Third and Fourth Years
in Mozambique,
September 2012–August 2014

Chapter 20
Walking in the Vision

"Jesus took . . . them up a high mountain." —
Mark 9:2, NIV

GOING TO MOZAMBIQUE, WE HAD low expectations of what we might achieve. We would be there less than five years, a relatively short time. There were language and culture barriers. We had previously visited Burkina Faso with the prospect of working with the Fulani—another Muslim "unreached" people group. The missionary family had been serving there faithfully for twenty years. Only as they were preparing to leave were they beginning to see the fruit of three young people committed to "following Jesus." Realistically, we thought we would be planting seeds and watering seeds our teammates had planted. We did not expect to see the fruit of people giving their lives to Christ—that would likely come later, after others had taken our place.

Once we arrived, however, I repeatedly felt the Spirit telling me "you will see fruit." I was afraid to share those feelings with anyone but Steve, but we tried to walk in that vision. We both prayed daily for wisdom and discernment. We meditated each morning on God's Word in our separate quiet times and we ended each day together in prayer. I prayed more in Mozambique than I had ever prayed before. I needed to pray. I knew I was totally dependent on God. We also knew that others were praying for us, and it was a good feeling.

So when we came back to the States in October of 2012 for a three-month furlough, we were on a mountain high, having seen unexpected fruit. We were walking in that mountain top vision. As we had the opportunity to speak to supporting churches and individuals, we asked for prayers for Miséria and the persecuted church.

Our furlough time flew by, the travel was tiring but it was wonderful to reconnect with family. We spent time with our children and granddaughters and got to meet our first grandson, Finn. We also spent time with my parents, sisters, nieces, and great nephews, Hayden and Brody. Hayden had recently lost his father, whose life was cut tragically short. I was thankful to have the opportunity to encourage him and reassure him of God's love at that critical juncture in his life—we've shared a special bond since that time.

We were still on the mountain when we returned to Mozambique at the end of December. On our way back, we stayed in Johannesburg long enough to purchase a submersible pump. We needed it for the borehole that had been drilled and capped just before we left for furlough. We put it in our luggage along with over sixty meters of electrical wire. Amazingly, it passed right through security and customs. Steve installed it soon after we got back and living in the village became much easier. We now had electricity, kitchen cabinets, and cold running water! We still heated our bathwater on the stove for our bucket baths, but we had grown accustomed to that. It dawned on me that most people in the world have never taken a hot shower or luxuriated in a bathtub of warm water. Consequently, I got over feeling sorry for myself about the bucket baths. Of course we did enjoy our hot showers while on furlough!

God was also blessing our marriage. With our teammates gone, Steve and I had to look to God and to each other even more than we had before. We felt grateful for each other's gifts. We were gifted differently, but our gifts complemented each other. Before we came, I knew Steve had an encyclopedic knowledge of Scripture (I call him my walking concordance). I also knew he had a lot of practical skills from being raised on a farm. But I never realized his skill set would include everything we needed to build a home and survive in the village. He designed our home, built it, and put in the plumbing and electricity. He built the cabinets using impressive carpentry skills. My respect for him increased greatly. I realized that in our previous life, I had failed to give him the respect he deserved—I felt bad about that.

I also admired the way Steve worked with the young men. He hired our neighbors—Idrissa, Abudu, and Assumane—to help him finish out the house. They had no experience, but he taught them these same skills with kindness, respect, and patience. He treated our guards the same way.

Julio was giving Steve language lessons. Steve took time out to visit their family *machamba*. He hoed with them and helped them bring in their crops. He studied the Bible weekly with Cascão, teaching him the art of expository preaching, carefully dividing the Word of God. To that end, he had to teach him how to use a dictionary, to look up every word he did not fully understand. Cascão had a sweet, gentle spirit and was extremely bright, but only had a sixth-grade education. Many of the young men we knew did not have the love of an earthly father. With time, some of them would come to see Steve as their father.

We were past the halfway point of our five-year commitment. We discussed extending our commitment to six years. The ministry was just starting to bear fruit and we wanted to see it through. We wanted to see these new believers mature and become firm in their new faith. And now we felt certain that others would soon come to Christ. We dared to pray that a church would be established in Nomba before our time was up.

A few weeks later, God opened another door to the gospel. Before we had left for furlough, Steve and I paid a visit to the chief. It was our custom to let him know when we were leaving and when we would return. While we were there, we asked him if he would like a Proclaimer. He said yes. But when I was explaining to him how to use it, the speaker came on quite loudly. He almost panicked, asking me to please turn it down quickly. I could tell that he didn't want people to know about *this* gift. Even so, I encouraged him to listen to the Gospel of John with his family.

Soon after our return from furlough, Julio and I went to visit the chief to discuss our plans for the children's program. We were grieved to find him sick in bed, deathly ill, with a high fever. He had lost a lot of weight. Sores on his abdomen were draining pus. He said he couldn't keep any food down and was certain he was dying. He confessed to us that he never wanted to be chief. He said that some powerful people in the village had appointed him. These same people had expectations that he would show them favor in tribal land dealings, giving them the best land for the least money. But he wanted to help the poor and marginalized in the village. So he went against the powerful leaders and sold good land to the poor at a price they could afford. Now he said the leaders were angry and had put a curse on him. They wanted him to die so they could replace him with another, more compliant chief.

I told the chief that we were going to pray for him in the name of our Savior, Jesus Christ. We would pray that God would heal him and that no curse from his enemies would have any power over him. I also told him that *someday* he would indeed die, however, because we all do. He and I were both fifty years old, which was beyond the average life expectancy in Mozambique. No one but God knew if he had one day or many years left. I looked up and noticed the Proclaimer sitting on the table. I asked him if he had been listening to it. He said that he and his family had been listening to it together.

"I do not understand why people feel so strongly against Jesus. He only did *good* things. He taught His followers to do good things as well," the chief said with a sad look on his face.

I asked him if we could listen to John 14 together before we prayed. As we listened together, I prayed silently for God to open his heart to the truth. When the chapter ended, I said, "It is true that one day you are going to die. But Jesus says that He prepares a place in heaven for those who follow Him. You don't have to be afraid of dying if you follow Jesus with all your heart."

I didn't wait for his response. I took his hand with my right hand and Julio's hand with my left and began to pray. Then Julio followed with a fervent prayer to our Lord. I felt God's presence, and a peace settled over us in that room. The chief's wife was moved to tears and thanked us for praying. She said she loved listening to God's word, it gave her a longing in her heart.

I went to town the next day and purchased some yogurt from a missionary friend who had a dairy. I took the yogurt and some papaya latex/saline mix and garlic oil to the chief's house. When I arrived he was sitting up in bed, tired, but with a smile on his face. His wife told me the fever broke shortly after we had left the previous day and he was doing much better. I left her the medicine and explained to her how to treat his wounds. I prayed with them again and went home.

The next week, Julio and I returned and found him up and about, eating a big plate of chicken and rice. He said God had healed him and he was getting strong again. We gathered around and said a prayer of thanksgiving to God. I felt the floodgates were about to open and God would pour out His spirit in Nomba.

Chapter 21
Coming down the Mountain

THINGS WERE DEFINITELY LOOKING UP in the early part of 2013, but not everything was good. I had given Abamia more responsibility in the orphan program when I was treating Lucia and discovered he had been untrustworthy. I gave him a chance to repent but he would not, even after I confronted him with the evidence. So I told him we could no longer work together, because I could not work with someone who was not truthful. Afterward, he tried his best to sabotage the program but, thankfully, he was not successful.

We heard about a series of armed robberies, also called "home invasions," occurring with increasing frequency across Northern Mozambique. Two families from our Good News for Africa team had been attacked. One of the families lived in Nampula. The other family lived in the small town of Montepuez near the east coast.

Closer to home, two missionary families in the Lichinga district had been attacked in recent months. We were friends with both families. They were badly shaken. In both cases a gang of six to eight men with machetes came during the night, broke into the home, and terrorized family members while demanding money and electronics. Both families had small children. One of the husbands was beaten severely with iron rods.

We already had horizontal bars on our windows. When we learned of the robberies, Steve added vertical bars to the windows and iron cages to the front and back doors. Our beautiful home looked more like a prison, and it depressed me. We left the doors open during the day but locked ourselves in at dusk. We asked each of our guards to choose another man to work with them so there would always be two guards at night. Our guards were pleased with the security upgrades. They especially appreciated that we allowed them to choose a man they trusted for the work. By that time, we had already fired Lukia's husband, Emilio. He was using his salary on another woman instead of caring for Lukia and the children. We had hired a man named Omar to replace him. Omar chose his brother Louis, and Samuel chose his friend Carlito. All the men received stern warnings that they were to take care of their wives and children with their salary, or we'd fire them too.

We hired the extra men none too soon. The very next night a gang of six men armed with machetes showed up. We woke up to a ruckus when they met fearless Samuel and Carlito head on. Our guards were outnumbered but one managed to blow the whistle. Several of our neighbors came running, and the thieves fled.

The next day, Steve went back to work. He rigged a flood light outside our bedroom window and a loud car horn that we could turn on with a flip of a switch next to the bed. He also made a spear for each guard by filing down a machete blade to a sharp point, then attaching it to a pole. We called a meeting with all our guards and our neighbors. We showed them the newest improvements so they would know what the car horn meant. Everyone was very impressed, delighted even. We thanked our neighbors who had come to our aid the night before and gave them sacks of rice as a small token of our appreciation. We really couldn't thank them enough, because they probably saved Samuel and Carlito's lives as well as our own by their quick response. We felt very blessed to be a part of that community.

It was a stressful time. The day that is emblazoned in my memory, however, is the day Miséria showed up at our house, not long after our return. She said she had told her persecutors, "You can kill me with an axe; you can kill me with a machete. You can burn me to death in my own home. *But I'm going to follow Jesus and be baptized!*"

And she was baptized. Afterward, though, we all quickly descended into the valley.

Chapter 22
Walking through the Valley

THERE WAS THE "USUAL" STUFF of Mozambique in 2013: snakes, thieves, and harassment from the government. What hurt the most, however, was watching my spiritual child be persecuted, not knowing how it would end. I had grown very, very close to Miséria. We had spent many months together treating Lucia. Miséria studied the Bible with us every week, and I was also giving her weekly reading lessons. Nevertheless, I felt totally inadequate to speak to her about persecution because I had never experienced it.

I remember sharing some passages with her from 1 Peter. As we finished reading, the Spirit prompted me to tell her "If they ever *lay hands* on you—flee!" She did just that one day soon afterward when her husband attacked her as she was preparing to take a bath. She had no clothes on when he came in, threw her telephone into the latrine, and began to beat her. She escaped his grasp, and ran several miles through the villages of Nomba, Lumbe Dois, and Chenganani to Jon's house wearing nothing but a cotton cloth that she managed to grab on her way out.

Jon called and told us what had happened. We brought her some clothes and toiletries and asked her what we could do for her. She asked us to give her a ride to her daughter's house, on the other side of Nomba, where she thought she would be safe.

Although she had several grown children, she still had a twelve-year-old and a six-year-old living at home, so she didn't want to be far from them. We dropped her off but didn't feel she would be safe there. We advised her that, if he came looking for her, she needed to flee to the house of Asainabo, Julio's mother, in Ntoto, where her husband wouldn't think to go looking for her.

That same evening, her husband came looking for her at their daughter's home. She heard him speaking to neighbors as he approached. She snuck out to Guida's house next door and asked Guida to hide her. Her husband suspected Guida as well because she was also studying the Bible with us, and went to her house next. Guida met him at the gate and told him she had just seen Miséria running back to their house. As soon as he was out of sight, Miséria snuck out and fled to the village of Ntoto, about four miles in the opposite direction. She arrived under the cover of darkness and lived several days with Asainabo, who had gone through a similar experience when she came to Christ.

The following morning we learned from Julio what had happened. I gathered some extra food and clothes for Miséria and went to Ntoto. That is when I experienced a sweet time of worship with the persecuted church. It is a memory I cherish and one I would have missed, had we not gone to Mozambique. As we were sitting in her house, one by one, each of Asainabo's grown sons and daughters, who were also Christians, came in the room. They began to share the suffering that they endured when they came to Christ. They were the only Christians in that village. Then, one of them broke out into a song of praise, and another followed, and another—then came a time of prayer. It was all spontaneous. The Holy Spirit's presence was heavy in that place. A scripture came to mind. "If you are reviled for the name of Christ, you are blessed because the Spirit of glory and of God rests on you" (1 Pet. 4:14).

As the months wore on and the persecution continued, Miséria stayed strong, but I began to waver. I felt guilty about her suffering, afraid she might be martyred. I talked to her about it one day. I asked her if she was glad she had decided to follow Jesus now that she'd lost so much. She answered simply, "I am free now." I knew she was in God's hands, and I had peace after that.

The peace did not last long, however, because our relationship with Benne had already begun to deteriorate. He became increasingly antagonistic—abusing the workers and stealing from the center. He was managing the center as a private business in the typical top-down, authoritarian style of colonial Mozambique.

I was riding my bike through the village one day and stopped by the center to see Miséria. Xandra had recently quit working at CSJ and a new shepherd was bringing in the goats. I immediately noticed that roughly two-thirds of the goat herd had twine tied around their necks. I asked the shepherd about the twine. He told me that Benne had gone through the herd the previous day and placed twine on most of the goats. Benne told him that the goats with twine were now his *personal* goats. He instructed the shepherd to separate them from the rest of the herd each night and put them into a pen in Benne's yard. Benne had recently built a high brick wall with a solid iron gate around his yard. The wall was topped with broken pieces of glass embedded in the cement to keep thieves from climbing over.

I had been caring for the goat herd for three years and knew them quite well. I was never told that Benne owned any of them personally, certainly not two-thirds of the herd. I also noticed that the best goats had the twine and only the sickly, infertile, and older goats were left for CSJ. I inquired as to Benne's whereabouts, and the shepherd told me that he had already left for the day.

I proceeded to the kitchen; Miséria was not there. I asked one of the other workers and they told me she had not come in that day because she was sick. So I rode on to Miséria's house to check on her. I found her in bed. When I asked her what was wrong, she burst into tears. She said she could not face Benne because of the terrible things he had said to her the previous day.

Miséria's nephew had been badly burned. She told her brother to bring the child to the center so she could treat him. When they arrived, she took money out of her own pocket to purchase aloe vera from the center for the child. She proceeded to clean the wounds and treat the child when Benne showed up. He chastised Miséria severely in front of everyone, bellowing, "Who do you think you are, treating that child? *You* are not a doctor. *You* are not a nurse. *You* never even went to school. *You* can't even read. *You are nothing, and you know nothing!*"

My anger burned as I put my arm around Miséria to comfort her, wishing I could take away those awful words. She burst into tears again, covering her face with her hands and sobbed. "*Mamãe* it is not my fault that I can't read. *You* know my story. *You* know how my father was murdered and my mother went insane when I was just a child. *You* know how I was sent away, how I had to work, how they treated me. *You* know I never got the chance to go to school."

Every ounce of self-esteem Miséria had gained by studying the Bible and successfully treating Lucia had been stolen by

Benne in that one encounter. I swallowed hard to gain my own composure as I grasped her shoulders with both my hands. When she raised her head, and her eyes met mine, I emphatically told her, "Miséria, *You* are the daughter of the King, the most high God! *He loves you with an everlasting love.* No matter what Benne or anyone else says, *nothing* will ever change that!"

I let my words sink in before I continued. "What Benne did was wrong. He never should have spoken to you that way. But your value is as a child of God, not what Benne thinks of you. We need to try to forgive him. We need to pray that God will help us to forgive him and that he will repent and turn back to God."

Miséria's tears subsided as she slowly nodded her head. I took both her hands in mine and we prayed together for the grace to forgive Benne. I think I needed that grace more than she did. I felt the anger of a mother when someone wounds her child. I prayed that God would comfort Miséria and heal the deep wounds that Benne's hateful words had cut into her heart.

I went home that night and told Steve what had happened. He was also grieved to the core for Miséria's sake and saddened that Benne had taken such an evil turn. We took time over the next few days to confirm both Miséria's story and that of the shepherd before confronting Benne or sharing it with the other board members. It did not take long to get confirmation. Everyone had been present when he railed on Miséria. Benne himself had announced to the entire crew that the goats with string around their necks were his. Several of the old crew had recently quit because of Benne's abusive behavior or been fired after they objected to it.

I went to Xandra to ask him if any of the goats were truly Benne's. I knew he would know since he was with CSJ from the beginning. I reasoned that he would tell me the truth without fear since we had a good relationship and he no longer worked for Benne. Xandra told me that four years ago, Benne had purchased four goats of his own and kept them with the CSJ herd. At that time, it amounted to less than one-quarter of the herd. The center bore the costs of feeding and caring for Benne's goats. Xandra said that every time a goat got sick and died, Benne would say it was not one of his goats, even if it wasn't true. Xandra knew exactly which goats were Benne's and which goats belonged to CSJ. Benne had claimed more than twice as many as were truly his. Xandra then proceeded to tell me the name and pedigree of each goat that Benne owned. People made fun of Xandra's lack of sophistication, but that man knew his goats!

When we spoke to Jon, he confirmed Benne's abusive behavior toward Miséria and related yet another incident involving the goats. A few months before Benne had separated the herd, four goats had been stolen. Benne was going to take money out of the guard's salary to replace the goats. Jon knew the guard would go hungry. He was a poor and elderly man; it would take him many months to pay for the goats. So Jon suggested all the members take an equal portion out of their salaries to help cover the cost. Everyone agreed. Over the next few months, Benne collected the money from the others and kept it in the safe. In the meantime, he had put the strings on the goats' necks. Then, after he collected the full value of the stolen goats, he told the others, "The goats that were stolen were also *my* goats. But I don't need any more goats, so I am just going to keep this money."

Jon said he never would have suggested they raise money to replace the goats if he had known Benne was going to keep the money for himself. All the other employees confirmed Jon's story and said they felt the same way.

We called a board meeting and confronted Benne about the goats and his treatment of Miséria. He claimed the goats were his. He said that all of *his* goats were very fertile and healthy. They always had twins and never got sick. Only the CSJ goats had died or were barren over the last four years. Furthermore, he claimed that everyone knew that the stolen goats were his and that he would get the money. He said they were all *happy* to give him the money. As for Miséria, he was only *protecting* her. He didn't want her to get in trouble with the authorities for treating sick people.

We wanted to discipline Benne with a temporary suspension from his position as manager of CSJ. Unfortunately, we didn't have the votes. The board was divided exactly in half with Benne and all his friends and family members taking his side, and an equal number of outside board members and CSJ members opposing him. We contacted our absentee team members for support to break the tie. Drew responded but suggested part of the problem was a personality conflict with Jon. He reminded Benne of the statutes and, in the end, said we needed to find a way forward, but did not offer his vote. Thomas never responded at all.

After months of agonizing over the situation in prayer, first encouraging and later admonishing Benne to repent, the situation finally got so bad that we felt we had no choice but to separate ourselves from the organization. We did not want the community to think we approved of his behavior or that what he was doing was Christian behavior. We explained to the chief what we were about to do and why we were doing it. He went with us to CSJ and told Benne to gather the entire crew for a meeting. We relayed to everyone why we were resigning from the board and handed Benne a formal letter of resignation. We told the rest of the staff that we still loved them and cared for them. They would always be welcome in our home.

After we left, we were told that Benne became furious. He threatened the employees that no one was to speak to us. He also said he was going to write a letter to the government to get us kicked out of the country. He claimed that since we were sent there to help him, we needed his approval to stay.

Ignoring his threats, Miséria came and told us everything that had happened. We went separately to Jon who confirmed Miséria's story. Soon afterward, Benne pressured Jon into resigning by telling him that if he did not quit, he would fire everyone else. Benne threatened Jon because Jon was on the board of directors and, according to the statues, he could not be fired by Benne. Jon, of course, did not want the others to lose their livelihood and complied.

The next week, we were informed by a friend that we were being investigated by the secret police. She said we needed to be very careful about everything we said or did or with whom we were seen. She was frightened and made me promise to tell no one that she had told us. She was friends with the wife of the head of the secret police. That was how she found out about the investigation.

It was an anxious time for us. It was late July and our resident visas were going to expire in less than a month. We knew Benne was trying to get us kicked out of the country. Getting a foreigner kicked out was not difficult in Mozambique. The government is naturally suspicious of foreigners, plus there is extreme corruption. It would not take much of a bribe to have our visas canceled.

We were worn down by that time. We prayed a lot and finally gave it up to the Lord. We agreed, "If we get kicked out, we get kicked out—He is in control." We continued to do our work in the various ministries and tried not to think about it.

Several days after the investigation began, the chief came up to me one Saturday when I was working with the children at the primary school. We had one of those conversations—common when you are working in a foreign language and culture. You understand the words a person is saying but you don't know if you understand the hidden meaning *behind* the words. It went like this:

"We like the work you are doing here. It is good work," the chief began.

"Thanks!" I replied.

"We want you to stay here," he continued.

"That's good, because we really want to stay!"

"So, I wrote you a good report."

"Report? What report?" I asked.

"The report I had to put in *the book*," he explained.

"The book? What book?"

"The *book* where *they* put the reports. I wrote you a good report to put in the book, because *we want you to stay*," he said slowly and emphatically.

"Great!" I responded with equal emphasis to indicate that I understood his meaning, "Thank you very much for writing us a good report—*we want to stay*."

Chapter 23
A Respite and a Special Blessing from the Lord

TWO WEEKS AFTER MY CONVERSATION with the chief about the mysterious book and report, God blessed me again with another encounter during the children's program. We were singing praise songs in the primary school classroom. The classroom had doorways but no doors. Likewise, it had windows but no glass, and it also lacked desks and chairs. It was the perfect place to meet with seventy or so children! A beautiful young lady slipped in while we were singing. She smiled shyly at me and curtsied slightly as is the Yao custom in showing respect. I didn't stop singing but motioned her to come in and join us, thinking she was a curious onlooker from the village. Having no windows or doors allowed for frequent guests whom we always welcomed.

We continued singing several more songs, and the young woman sang along with us in the back corner of the large room. Then she smiled and curtsied again before walking back out the door. It was only after she left that my memory was jarred. I thought, *That young lady looks a lot like Lucia. Dear Lord, could it be Lucia, back after all this time?*

Over a year had passed since Lucia left us and we had all but given up on her return. A panic seized me as I thought I might have let Lucia slip in and out of my life again without recognizing her, not knowing how to find her again. The woman was already across the school yard, about to disappear into the maze of huts. I knew I wouldn't be able to catch her even if I ran after her. I quickly prayed a silent prayer, *Dear Lord, if that is Lucia, please let her turn around and come back to me!*

The woman suddenly stopped, turned around, and headed back in our direction. When she stood in the doorway the second time, smiling her shy smile, I said, "Lucia, is that *you*?"

"Yes, *Tia*, it is me," she said as she broke into a huge smile and pulled a necklace out from her blouse, as if for proof. It was the necklace I had given her with the fish and the cross.

Laughter, hugs, and kisses followed as the children looked on with curiosity at our joyous reunion. Lucia had gained several pounds since I had seen her last and even had dimples in her cheeks. She appeared to be about three months pregnant as well. I asked her if she would give her testimony to the children about what God had done for her.

As Lucia told her story to the normally rambunctious group of children, you could have heard a pin drop in that room. She told them about the fire and the extent of her and Ana's injuries. She said she felt she had already died and that she was cursed by God. She wished she would die. "But then these people, *Tia* and Miséria, came and told me that Jesus loved me and could heal me. I did not believe them at first, but they kept coming and treating me and praying for me. Another lady, named Teresa, who had been struck by lightning, came with them one day and told me how Jesus had healed her. They all prayed for me and I began to believe their words. So I prayed for Jesus to heal me, and look what He did! I was as good as dead," she exclaimed, "but look at me now. I can walk. I can hoe. I can even dance!"

With that, she broke into a dance for the Lord as the children clapped and cheered. It was a powerful witness to the children. We were always telling them that God really is good, one hundred percent of the time. Yet Lucia's testimony was better than a thousand exhortations from me. She was living proof of His compassion and mercy.

After the program was over, I accompanied Lucia back to *Anganga's* home and we called Miséria to join us. Together we prayed a prayer of thanksgiving to the Lord. Over the next several weeks, Lucia went about the village telling her story to anyone who would listen.

I was scheduled to teach about using plant medicine as a way to share the love of Jesus at the YWAM center in a neighboring village later that month. I had already asked Miséria to join me in teaching and giving practical demonstrations of the techniques. I asked Lucia and Teresa to come give their testimonies to the students as well. They did, and it made an enormous impact. Several of the women in that class began to use the techniques. It opened doors to the gospel for them, much as it had for us.

August arrived. It was time, once again, to apply for our visas to be renewed. With all that had happened in the previous six months, we could only prepare for the worst and hope for the best. In the weeks leading up to the deadline for renewal, I found myself making a mental checklist of the most important things to do if we had to leave the country on short notice. Thankfully, that wasn't necessary because that year our visas were actually renewed with fewer difficulties than usual—no doubt, due to the good report that the chief put in "the book."

Although it began well, 2013 turned out to be the most diffi-cult time of spiritual warfare that we experienced in Mozambique. It was no coincidence that evil forces were stirred up into high gear, because the Spirit was really moving. More people joined the Bible study, and more people came to Christ. In November, we asked Cascão and his wife Merina, Jon and his wife Carolina, Miséria, Julio and his mother Asainabo, if they would like to work together to plant a church in Nomba. They all responded with joyful enthusiasm in spite of the persecution that would be sure to follow. In December a small body of believers met together as a church for the first time in Nomba village.

"In everything give thanks; for this is God's will for you in Christ Jesus" (1 Thess. 5:18).

Miséria and Asainabo taught us to how praise God in the valley that year. Oswald Chambers wrote that we are not meant to stay on the mountain, for it is in the valley that we live for the glory of God. It is there that our faithfulness is revealed accord-ing to our personal relationship with Jesus.[19]

Will we be faithful, believing in His character, or will we deny Him? It is in the valley, we cry out, "Lord, I believe; help my unbe-lief!" (Mark 9:24).

---

[19] Taken from *My Utmost for His Highest®* by Oswald Chambers, edited by James Reimann, © 1992 by Oswald Chambers Publications Assn., Ltd., and used by permission of Discovery House, Grand Rapids MI 49501. All rights reserved.

Chapter 24
Chinonyelo Cha Isa

DECEMBER 1, 2013, FELL ON a Sunday. We gathered that morning outside of Cascão's tiny house and sat in a circle on mats, stools, and a few chairs. I counted fourteen adults, including myself, Steve, and six members from the house church in Chenganani. Twenty children of various ages sat on the mats in the center of the circle.

Steve recited Hebrews 10:23–25 about the importance of meeting together. Then Jon opened with a time of prayer, which was intermingled with songs of praise and worship. The first song we sang was one I knew well from the children's program: *"Chinonyelo Cha Isa"* which means "The Love of Jesus" in Chiyao. The translated words are:

"The love of Jesus is very powerful. Look there! Jesus died on the cross."

"Why did He die?"

"He died so we could have life! The love of Jesus is powerful!"

The worship was spontaneous with different members leading a song or praying out loud as the Spirit moved them, and yet, it was orderly with each one waiting to take his or her turn. I was happy to note that the women also participated well. After some time, Jon read a passage from Matthew and expounded on "Who Jesus is to us who believe." This is a crucial matter of understanding for believers coming from a Muslim background because Islam maintains that Jesus was a prophet only, not the Son of God.

Then we began sharing various scriptures and stories on our hearts. That is when Jon's son-in-law, a young man named Mendes, quoted Acts 2:17. "And it shall be in the last days . . . that I will pour out My Spirit on all mankind; and your sons and daughters shall prophesy, and your young men shall see visions and your old men shall dream dreams . . ."

Mendes then recounted a dream he'd had the previous night. He dreamed that we all had come to Nomba to worship just as we were doing. Then some imams and other leaders of the mosque, as well as some government officials, showed up. They forbade us to worship and establish a church here. Then the government official took a national flag and set it in the ground. After that, the imam took a flag of Islam and set it next to the government flag. The imam then began to read from the Quran, after which he took out a small book of curses and began putting curses on us. We resisted, however, and said "In the name of Jesus, these curses will not affect us. We claim this place for Christ and we will worship here!" Then we put up the flag of Christ and began again to worship—and the dream ended there.

After Mendes finished, Miséria gave a testimony. An imam had showed up at her house the previous week. From ten a.m. to three p.m. he interrogated her about her faith, quoting passages from the Quran, and pressuring her to turn back to Islam. She said she prayed in her heart for God to give her the correct responses from His Word that she had stored up in her heart. "And He did!" she exclaimed. "God gave me a scripture for every argument the imam had."

The imam finally stood up and told Miséria's brother and husband, "This one will never turn back." And with that, he left.

As Miséria was telling the story, I looked up just as the sun was breaking through the clouds, and saw a dove fly over our little group. It happened in an instant, but it is another image from Mozambique that is forever imprinted in my memory.

After more testimonies, Steve read a passage about the significance of the sacrament of communion, and James—the eldest son of Jon—led us in prayer before we took the Lord's Supper. There were more spontaneous prayers of thanksgiving. Then Jon took off his cap and laid it on the mat and said that whoever was able to, should give an offering. Almost everyone gave something despite their material poverty and the equivalent of eleven dollars was collected. Guida prayed over the offering. The amount was counted and recorded in front of everybody. Jon nominated Miséria to be treasurer and guard the collection until they all decided how they might use it when there was a need.

We concluded with a prayer of thanksgiving and another song. It was a beautiful time, and Steve and I were blessed beyond measure to be a part of it.

Chapter 25
Difficult Choices

December, January, and February can be difficult
months for the peasant farmer in Mozambique. It is the height
of the rainy season. Many families literally move out of the village for several months each year and live at their *machambas*
in makeshift huts that may be twenty miles or more from their
home in the village. Going back and forth every day takes too
much time and energy, when traveling by foot or bicycle.

The families start preparing their fields for planting in
November, making harrows by hand with a hoe. Once the rains
begin in earnest, they plant corn and hoe the weeds carefully until the corn reaches at least knee-high. Then they may also plant
some beans, if they have the resources to do so. Meanwhile, the
food from the crop they harvested last year may be running low
or already be gone. Because supplies are so low, the prices for corn
soar. Consequently, the peasants do the hardest work of the year
having consumed the least amount of food. Sometimes they don't
have enough cash to buy other necessities like salt, oil, and soap.

Malaria flourishes that time of year. People go untreated, because their fields are too far from the health clinics. The heavy
rains make traveling difficult. Sometimes every member of the
household will end up being sick. Once the first person comes

down with the disease, the mosquitos spread it from one victim to the next. Even if they do make the journey back to the village, they might not get treatment. Sometimes the health posts run out of malaria medicine due to the high demand. Additionally, as the level of the ground water rises in the village, cross contamination between the water wells and the latrines occurs. The result is waterborne illness, like cholera. Everybody suffers.

$\approx$

I stopped by to visit Lukia one day in January. She had recently returned from her *machamba*. She was starting a new field, far from the village, that had never been planted. Consequently, the work was extra strenuous. Normally the husband does the work of clearing a new field, and the wife does the work of planting and hoeing, or both work together. Lukia and Emilio, however, continued to have problems in their marriage.

We had to make the difficult decision to fire Emilio the previous year. Instead of examining his own culpability regarding courting other women and not providing for his family, Emilio blamed Lukia. He reasoned that if she had not told us about the suffering of her and the children, we would not have found out. To the contrary, however, I had already seen it with my own eyes before she ever said a word.

Lukia had planned to live out at the *machamba* with the children until it was time for school to start in February. Then they would return to the village and she would rest a week before going back to work the *machamba*. When she returned, she planned to leave her two school-age children in the village with Emilio and take the two youngest children back with her. I was proud of her for making that difficult choice to leave the older kids even though she needed their help. She wanted to keep them in school so their future would be brighter than her own.

By the time they got back, however, they had all come down with malaria. Bwana and Judit had gotten sick first, and Lukia used the last of the artemisia tea I had sent with her to treat them. Despite her small stature, Lukia was incredibly tough. So when she said, "*Dada*, I'm really feeling bad, can you give me a ride to the hospital?" I knew she was very sick.

We went to the closest health post, and it was overflowing with people waiting, but at nine a.m., when no medical personnel had showed up, we went on to the hospital in Lichinga. It was also overflowing with people, but at least the staff were present. I left her with baby Judah and another neighbor lady riding with us who also had malaria. They waited all morning, and I finally got a call to pick them up in the afternoon. After we were back home, I found out they did get tested confirming that all three had malaria, but the hospital was out of medicine to treat it. Lukia spent her last bit of cash buying some medicine for the baby at a private pharmacy, but she didn't have any money left to buy medicine for herself. I did not learn this from Lukia. The other lady told me about it in private so as not to shame Lukia.

Lukia was weak and burning up with fever. I still had one course of malaria meds left at the house, so I immediately brought them to Lukia and gave her the first dose. I was fearful she was going to slip out of consciousness. By the next day, all the hospitals and private pharmacies were completely out of malaria meds. I know, because I went to each one hoping to refill my own supply.

I tell this story as a testimony that Lukia loves and cares for her children as best as she can with her meager resources. One might think otherwise when I describe what happened two weeks later. I stopped by to visit again knowing Lukia would soon be returning to her *machamba*. It was lunchtime and Emilio was eating his *xima* with some beans. Lukia and the four children were waiting until he finished, then they would eat the leftovers. I had never noticed this custom before, so I asked her, "Is this the way it always is? The man eats first, and then the wife and children?"

She looked down with an amused smile at my lack of understanding and said, "No, *Dada*, when we have plenty of food we all eat together. It is just when we have little food that we do it this way."

I watched as Emilio brought out a small bowl of beans for his wife and children to share. I excused myself quickly lest she offer me some of the beans.

As Lukia escorted me half way back to our house, as was her custom, I thought about Jesus' words about the humility of a child, and how the kingdom of God belongs to such as these.

We arrived at our property boundary, turned and faced each other, holding hands. Lukia told me she was strong now and would be returning to the *machamba* with Judah and Aida. She saw the concern in my eyes and said, "Don't worry. We've got some pumpkin out there we can eat with our early corn."

"What about Bwana and Judit?" I asked.

"They will just eat the *farelo*,[20] and their father will eat the corn flour. We don't have any other food left, unless their father manages to buy some more beans."

---

[20] *Farelo* is a coarse meal made from the outer husk of the kernel. It is the byproduct produced when the grain is milled and is usually fed to livestock.

"Sister," I said, "tell the children not to go hungry while you are gone. Tell them to visit their *tia* often, and I will make them some good food."

The kids did visit me a few times a week. Knowing their diet was deficient of quality protein I always cooked them eggs, but I knew they went to bed hungry most nights. Anything I gave them as a family, Emilio would keep for himself. Bwana trapped sparrows to eat and a termite invasion was a blessing[21].

It was a terrible time knowing they were going hungry, wishing I could make things right, but being unable to do so.

---

21   The Yao considered termites a delicacy when fried in oil with a little salt. The hungry children, however, ate them raw as quickly as they could catch them.

Chapter 26
The Fruitful Fourth Year

SOON AFTER MISÉRIA HAD BECOME a believer, she begged us to start a Bible study in her home. She wanted her family to learn about Jesus. Cascão and Merina lived only a few houses down from Miséria's house and in between the two houses was a mosque. Nomba is a large village with several mosques, but this mosque was one of the larger ones. We didn't think it was wise to meet there due to the proximity of the mosque and the fact that we used an audio Bible played at a rather high volume. Nevertheless, against our better judgement, we began to meet at her home on Wednesday nights. The leaders of the mosque were soon provoked and began threatening Miséria again. They also threatened to burn our truck. We were not threatened directly, but they delivered the threats through rumors passed on to participants of the Bible study, so we would be sure to find out.

We sought another place to hold the study. We did not want to use our own home for the Bible studies or worship, because we did not want the church to be viewed as "ours" (and consequently, cease to exist when we left). At that time, Guida was a seeker but not yet a believer. She volunteered her house, which was close to our side of the village.

Once our dog Nando figured that out, he began crashing the meetings, causing quite a disturbance. Guida's family was used to him, but most of the villagers were afraid of dogs, especially a big dog like Nando. We had to start locking him in our home Wednesday evenings before we left to keep him from following us. Nando hated being left behind and soon learned to recognize Wednesdays by whatever signals we inadvertently gave. He would invariably "go missing" on Wednesday afternoons, only to show up again at Guida's house that night. We eventually reached a compromise by teaching him to lie quietly in the corner of the yard.

When the Bible study was being held at Miséria's home, Guida's attendance had been irregular. As a single mother of six children, she was frequently unable to attend. Once we began to meet in her home and she was hearing the Word on a regular basis, however, it began to cut her heart. Her ten-year-old daughter, Melody, was in the children's program and already knew the stories from Creation to the birth of Jesus by heart. I was glad she and her younger siblings would now begin to hear more about the teaching and ministry of Jesus.

After several months, things had calmed down at Miséria's house. Several new seekers were coming on Wednesday evenings. So we decided to split the group and begin a second listening group on Friday nights at Miséria's house for the new seekers, beginning again in the book of John. Cascão and Miséria would lead the study. Meanwhile, we also continued to meet on Wednesday nights at Guida's house, building on the foundation of the book of John. We asked Jon to lead that group.

Guida came from a prominent family on her mother's side. She was the niece of the queen of the village, Catarina. Catarina's mother, Guida's grandmother, was considered a matriarch of the village, to be greatly respected. Against the will of her family, Guida decided to follow Jesus and be baptized in the spring of 2014. Afterward, Guida's mother secretly confided to her that she was happy for her. She told Guida that she had wanted to follow Jesus when she was a young woman living in Nampula during the war. That was where she had met Guida's father, a Macua man, who was a Christian. He shared the gospel with her, and they were soon married. Guida's grandmother, however, did not approve of the marriage because the man was not a Muslim. She eventually coerced her daughter to leave her husband. Guida's mother then returned to Nomba with her children. Although she returned to Islam, she still longed for Jesus.

Earlier that year, Cascão had befriended a young man named Nelito, from the village of Mitava, and began to talk to him about Jesus. It wasn't long before Nelito was riding his bicycle several miles in the dark to join the Friday night listening group at Miséria's house. It was too dangerous for him to bring his beautiful wife, Paulina, but Nelito would share what he learned with her each time he returned home. Soon the young couple began showing up with their baby to worship with us on Sundays.

Nelito and Paulina were also baptized that spring. Cascão baptized Nelito and then Paulina joined them in the lake and together they baptized Paulina. In a surprising move, Nelito then scooped up Paulina in his arms and carried her back to the shore. It was a joyous occasion to see the love this young family had for the Lord and for each other. Cascão and Merina also had this blessing. The hope that these two young families had would be manifested in the names they chose for their children, translated as follows: Hope, Peace, Happiness, and Sunshine.

Although Miséria longed for her husband to know Jesus, he refused to believe and eventually left her to marry another woman. Despite the suffering she had received at his hand, she was deeply saddened by his departure. Yet God blessed Miséria in other ways. She not only became adept at treating illnesses and injuries with plant medicines, but she also had the gift of healing through prayer alone.

One day, on her way home from Lichinga, Miséria came across a paralyzed man begging in the street. In a script straight out of the book of Acts, she told the man, "I have no money to give you, but I want to pray for you in the name of Jesus."

The man consented. Miséria laid her hands on him and prayed for God to heal him. The man was healed instantly and walked home rejoicing.

Another time, Lucia's mother-in-law, *Anganga,* brought one of her grandchildren to our worship service. She told us that she feared the child had been possessed by an evil spirit, because she frequently went into convulsions and would throw herself into the fire. At the end of the service, we gathered around *Anganga* and the child, who was listless at the time, and prayed over her. Nothing spectacular happened during the prayer, but *Anganga* later told us the child never had convulsions again. God had healed her through prayer alone.

Word began to spread. Under the cover of darkness, women would slip into our Friday night studies with their sick children, saying, "I heard that when this group prays over children they are healed."

Other women would come asking for prayers to be healed of infertility. That is how we met Mariamo. She was Miséria's neighbor and had heard of the miraculous healings of others. She told us she had been unable to conceive since her last daughter, Eva, was born seven years earlier. Miséria's response tickled me. She matter-of-factly told Mariamo, "Of course God can open your womb. He does that sort of thing all the time. But what is more important is that you know Him. We will pray for you, but you should stay and learn about Him."

Mariamo did stay and was soon coming every Friday night with Eva. God's word seemed to touch Mariamo's heart almost immediately. She became so hungry for more that she risked coming to our worship service one Sunday morning. Her family soon found out about it, and they threatened her life if she continued to study with us. We did not see her for almost a month. Then, one Friday night, she slipped in again. She spoke prophetically when she said, "The truth of God's Word has been hidden from us [Yao people] for so long, but now it is being revealed. Although I have been threatened for coming here, I must keep coming where I receive the Truth and gain understanding from God's Word."

Meanwhile, Julio continued to teach the children in the program. He also taught Bible stories to the children of the church on Sunday mornings before our regular worship time. Because we met outside, many curious children from the village and some women also showed up to hear the stories and learn the songs.

Cascão had a gift for teaching and preaching the Word with a gentle, loving spirit. His wife, Merina, had a bubbly, joyful spirit that shone brightly in her singing and prayers. They, along with Miséria and Asainabo, were constantly sharing the Good News of Jesus wherever they went. My heart was blessed by their courage and strong desire to share the love of Christ with those who did not yet know Him.

Soon, people in the village were beginning to ask them, "What church is this? Are you with the Catholics or the Anglicans?"

We had never talked to any of the believers about denominations. It was never our desire to establish a particular denomination. We just hoped to lead people to Christ and disciple them. We wanted them to worship God freely as the Spirit led them. So, when these questions were put to Cascão and the others, they did not know how to respond except that, "No, we are not Catholics or Anglicans, but we do follow Jesus."

People heard us open our time of worship most Sundays with "the Love of Jesus" song. They also heard us singing it with the children. So they asked Cascão, "Well, then, are you the *Chinonyelo Cha Isa* church?"

When Cascão relayed the story back to us, he asked us the name of our mission so that he would know what to tell people. We told him about the various protestant denominations, including our own, in the United States. Even so, we also told him that it was not our desire to impose a denomination on the new church. We felt denominations frequently divided believers instead of uniting them. As far as we were concerned, they were free to call themselves whatever they wished. Should they desire to register the church with the government, they could register as they wished. All we asked is that they adhere to the Bible as the inspired Word of God and continue to worship Jesus in Spirit and in truth. The church leaders met together without us and decided they would take the name *Chinonyelo Cha Isa* (The Love of Jesus). The name beautifully reflected their love for others.

The church elected to use the weekly offering to help families in need regardless of their religion. One of their first efforts was to help a Muslim family whose home had burned down. They lost everything, including their corn harvest. Church members brought them sacks of corn from their own harvest and purchased clothes for the children from the used clothing market in the city. The family was overwhelmed and somewhat mystified by this act of kindness. Other villagers took note as well, and doors were opened to the gospel. The number of seekers slipping in to the listening group on Friday nights swelled.

When she was not living at her *machamba*, Lukia was one of those who slipped in with her children.

Chapter 27

"By Me princes rule ... all who judge rightly."
—Proverbs 8:16

THE CHIEF OF NOMBA WAS a good man. The more I learned about him, the more I came to respect him. He and his wife lived in a house that was better than the average hut, but still modest, even by African standards. His home was a little more spacious, was made with fired bricks[22], and had a metal roof instead of thatch. He wasn't wealthy enough to own a car, but he did have a small motorcycle. In Mozambique, many people in positions of power—government officials, school teachers, and religious leaders—used their power to extort bribes to increase their wealth. To my knowledge, however, our chief never did such things. On the contrary, he worked very hard to provide for his family.

The chief worked as a nighttime guard at the main hospital in Lichinga. It was a dangerous job, but it earned him a regular salary. Additionally, he and his wife farmed a large *machamba* and garden. They sold their surplus produce to gain extra cash. Many

---

[22] Many of the huts in the village were made from unfired bricks because the family could not afford the cost of the firewood. These homes did not last as long and sometimes collapsed during the rainy season.

men did not help their wives much outside of planting and harvest times. The chief, however, could usually be found working with his wife in their *machamba* when he was not on duty at the hospital. He also carried out his duties representing the village and governing the villagers in all tribal affairs. To that effect, he acted to settle disputes within the village in order to keep the peace.

In the Yao culture, family disputes were first settled by the oldest brother or uncle. If possible, disputes between families were also settled this way. If that method did not resolve the issue, however, it could be brought to the chief, who would give counsel. The chief's counsel was usually heeded in honest disagreements, but one could go over his head to the court in Lichinga. Despite that, lawsuits were uncommon. In America, the rights of the individual are held in high esteem, and we have an abundance of lawyers to ensure our interests are protected. By contrast, in most African societies, the good of the tribe is ranked above the rights of the individual.

What endeared me most to the chief was the obvious love he had for his family. His wife was a lively, attractive woman. She only spoke Chiyao, and she spoke at a very rapid clip. I always had difficulty keeping up with her. She really wanted me to understand, however, so she would call on her husband or one of their grown children to translate to Portuguese if I was having too much trouble. She was from an influential family in the Lichinga district. Her uncle was the chief of Chiwaula, a large village on the outskirts of Lichinga. He was known as the "chief of the chiefs" of the outlying villages (including Nomba).

The chief and his wife married when she was only fifteen years old and he was twenty. In a culture where divorce and polygamy is common place, their marriage of over thirty years stood in stark contrast. He was certainly wealthy enough to take a second wife, and it was something of a status symbol to do so. Nevertheless, he chose instead to provide for the family he already had, and it was evident that God had blessed them with a happy marriage. He was also a skilled tailor[23] by trade, and he frequently sewed clothes for his wife and children. All of their children that I knew were sweet and respectful.

The chief was a head taller than the average Yao man, so he was easy to spot from a distance. I noticed him one day, walking home from the hospital in Lichinga, so I stopped to give him a ride. We chatted as I drove back to the village, and I eventually asked him if he was still listening to the Proclaimer.

"Yes, I am," he said with a grin. "A group of about forty people comes to my house on Friday afternoons, after prayers at the mosque, and we've been listening to the book of John. We are all the way to chapter 20!"

"Really!" I exclaimed, somewhat incredulous. "How did you convince forty people to come?" When we began, our groups were so small. We thought we were doing well to have ten people show up.

"You forget I'm the chief," he said with a laugh. "I told them to come, and they came."

All I could think was, *God, You are so good!* —knowing that His word does not go out without having its intended effect in the hearts of men.

I could not stop smiling for the rest of the day.

---

[23] In the Yao culture, tailors are almost exclusively men.

Chapter 28
Partnerships and
Matters of Culture

AFTER OUR TEAMMATES' DEPARTURE IN the spring of 2012, we became more proactive in seeking out informal partnerships with other missionaries in the Lichinga district. Many were doing a variety of wonderful works and we valued their fellowship, as well as their heart for the Yao people to know Jesus. We also appreciated the love and support we received from our other Good News for Africa teammates at our annual retreat, but they lived too far away to be of help on a regular basis.

We noticed that Youth with a Mission (YWAM) seemed to have a strong impact within the Yao culture. They had been established for some time in the area and had been a positive influence on both Jon and Julio. Fortunately, the YWAM center was located in the nearby village of Lumbe Dois. The Disciple Training School, which occurred yearly for the duration of five months, was held at that location. Students would come from other tribes in other provinces, and teachers would come from other countries. This helped the new believers to grasp how big and varied the kingdom of God is. It was a great encouragement to those who felt isolated if they were the only believer within their village or family.

The school would begin after harvest time in June and end at planting time in November. The first three months were class time. The basics of scripture and how it applied to topics like salvation, forgiveness, and marriage were taught from a Biblical world view. For new believers coming from a Muslim background, it was invaluable training. The last two months were a practical time during which the students learned to share their faith by working with other mission efforts and evangelizing in other communities and tribes.

The goals of the Disciple Training School complemented our work. Whenever possible, we raised funds for scholarships to enable new believers to take the course. For their part, the YWAM missionaries invited us to teach and preach at the school on several occasions. After the Nomba church was established, they sent students to work with us in the children's program and in evangelism campaigns.

The first ones we sent to the school were Cascão and Merina, the year following his conversion to Christianity. At the time, Merina was still a Muslim, but she decided to follow Christ after her second month at the school. YWAM allowed nonbelieving spouses to come if there was peace in the marriage. They would not allow a divided family to come, for instance, in a situation like Miséria's. The next year we were able to send Nelito and Paulina.

Another informal partner we worked with was Sending in Missions (SIM). Andrew and Tanya Smith were farmers from Australia before they came to Mozambique. Andrew's heart was to teach sustainable methods of farming from a Biblical world view. The hope was that the knowledge would help provide food security to the poor and also open doors to the Gospel of Jesus

Christ. We got to know the Smiths after our teammates left. They rented the Jackson's house from CSJ for a year while they were building a new house in an outlying district where they eventually planned to minister. Andrew employed Cascão part time to help him with the agriculture program and in the process, gave him some excellent training. The Smiths also joined us in worship when they lived in the village, and they fell in love with the Nomba church.

In their first year, the church had to grapple with several cultural issues. After worship one Sunday, Cascão said to the others, "What are we going to do about the ceremonies?"

The ceremonies he was referring to were traditional family celebrations to honor the ancestors at specific times after their death. Giving honor to the ancestors was a strong cultural value for the Yao. The problem was that during the ceremonies, sacrifices were made to the dead to gain their favor. Afterward, the family would feast on the food that had been offered up. Also, the spirits of the dead were sometimes invited to possess people in order to give them supernatural power. We did not know *all* that went on at these ceremonies, but I had treated several people for burns and injuries that had occurred when they were possessed by a "bad spirit." People talked about demon possession as matter-of-factly as we talk about heart disease and cancer in America.

The members of the church each offered recent experiences they'd had while trying to avoid participation in the ceremonies. I thought it telling that *all* felt that participation in the ceremonies violated their conscience. One man said he would not participate by bringing or eating the food, but he tried to show respect by offering to take the corn to the mill. Miséria said that she had sinned. She lied, telling them she could not participate because she was fasting that day. Guida said she violated her conscience by giving in to family pressure. She ate the food that had been sacrificed and was sick for three days afterward.

When they turned their eyes to us, expecting some words of wisdom, we told them that we could never know their culture well enough to tell them what to do. They would need to search the scriptures for themselves to determine which aspects of their culture were pleasing to God and which aspects were not. We advised that when they had to go against their culture, for the sake of their consciences, that they find another way to honor it that was pleasing to God.

Cascão then offered 1 Corinthians 10:20–21 as a reason they should abstain from the ceremonies. He read, ". . . the things which the gentiles sacrifice, they sacrifice to demons and not to God; and I do not want you to become sharers in demons. You cannot drink the cup of the Lord and the cup of demons; you cannot partake of the table of the Lord and the table of demons."

Everyone agreed, based on that scripture alone, that they should not participate in the ceremonies. But they were unable, on that day, to come up with a good way to show love and respect for the family of the deceased and honor their memory. Melody, Guida's eldest daughter, was sitting amongst the children that day, listening attentively to the discussion.

A few weeks later, Guida's grandmother showed up at Guida's house when she was not home. The grandmother had come to get the children so they could feast with her at a ceremony. When Melody realized the reason for her great-grandmother's visit, she quickly herded her younger siblings—Vania, Evaristo, and

Nandinho—into the house and locked the door. She told her great-grandmother they could not participate in ceremonies to the dead because it was not pleasing to God. Melody received a severe scolding through the door, but when she refused to come out, the grandmother finally gave up and left.

The grandmother found Guida later and severely chastised her for the way she was raising her children to disrespect their elders. Guida explained to her grandmother that they were not meaning to disrespect her, but they only wished to respect God. Her grandmother angrily responded that when Guida died, no one would bury her, and no one would honor her because of this. Guida replied, "It doesn't matter if they leave my body out in the street. I will already be in heaven with Jesus."

Another cultural tradition the church had to grapple with was *Unyago*, the initiation of children into adulthood and full membership into the tribe. Historically, children would go through *Unyago* around the time of puberty. In recent years, however, the age of children going through the ceremony was decreasing, some being as young as eight. The children went through *Unyago* in groups of their peers, and a special bond was formed between the participants. The groups of girls were usually housed in the village, while the boys were housed in long thatched huts, out in the bush. The boys were circumcised by a member of the tribe specifically designated and trained to perform the procedure. Then the children were kept in seclusion for one month. During that time, they were taught by various members of their families and the community about adulthood and what it means to be Yao.

At the end of their time of seclusion, the children washed themselves in the river. The thatched hut was burned, and an elaborate coming-out ceremony followed. The children received new clothes, sunglasses, and umbrellas and gathered together at one end of the village. Then they marched through the village as the rest of the villagers lined the streets. The children, now considered adults and full members of the tribe, had to keep a solemn expression as they passed through the cheering crowds.

Jacinta, my language teacher, was a good source of information about culture. I asked her to explain both the ceremonies and *Unyago* to me. I also asked others, within and outside of the church. While I typically received consistent answers regarding the ceremonies, I received a variety of answers regarding what the children were taught in *Unyago*. I concluded that while there were common threads, like circumcision of the boys and teaching respect for the elders, that ran through all *Unyago* ceremonies, they also varied widely depending on the family and community where they were held.

The missionary community likewise had widely divergent opinions about *Unyago*. Some believed it to be devoid of any redeeming value, and new believers should be encouraged not to allow their children to participate. Others thought that believers should develop a Christian version of *Unyago*. For our part, we felt that imposing our opinions on matters that we had limited knowledge about was unwise and possibly detrimental to the church. Also, we did not want them to rely on us for determining how to handle such matters. Instead, we encouraged them to wrestle with such matters before God and rely on His word. We trusted the Holy Spirit would guide them.

Two of Miséria's granddaughters were going through *Unyago* that year. She chose to fully embrace the tradition but to transform it with the love of Christ. Every day she showed up at the *Unyago* hut to teach the girls praise songs and stories from the Bible. People in the village said she was crazy for teaching them stories and songs that no one else knew. Even so, the girls learned well. After their coming-out celebration, they were soon teaching their families and friends, spreading joy throughout the village.

Chapter 29
Disillusion and Delusion

"Your wisdom and your knowledge, they have
deluded you . . ." —Isaiah 47:10

ALMOST A YEAR HAD PASSED since our formal resignation from the CSJ board of directors. Since then, we had not had much contact with CSJ aside from the occasional news we received from Miséria and others who still worked there. We were busy with our own ministries and, frankly, did not have the time or energy to worry about CSJ or Benne after we left. We continued to pray, for the sake of himself, his family, and his employees, that Benne would repent and turn back to God. Nevertheless, we did not feel called to continue to pursue him. We put him in God's hands and moved on. One day, Steve ran into Benne at central market and exchanged greetings. Benne told Steve he regretted that their relationship had not ended well. Steve replied, "Benne, your relationship with me is not what is important. What *is* important is your relationship with God. For the sake of your family and your own sake, you need to work on that relationship."

We never received any response from Drew or Thomas after our response to Drew's letter. We had plainly laid out the reasons why we felt CSJ could not continue to function as a Christian organization under Benne's leadership. Although we desired their input, when we did not hear back from them, we did what we thought was best. We knew they would be disappointed in the news. We even suspected that they, wanting to believe the best of Benne, might blame us for the problems. They had invested so much of themselves into the resource center and Benne personally, it was only natural that they would have a strong desire to see it succeed. The question was, though, what defined success?

To our limited knowledge, CSJ was succeeding well from a worldly point of view. Benne was clever and well educated. Additionally, he had business skills and a large amount of capital at his disposal. He was succeeding as a business man, expanding the assets of CSJ greatly since our departure. He was also expanding his personal wealth, building a large new house in Nomba and, we were told, he had also built a nice home in Malawi. There had been a high turnover amongst the CSJ workers, but the center continued to provide a livelihood for several families in the community and at least some of the original crew still worked there.

We still hoped that someday CSJ would function as a Christian organization. But regardless of whether that came to pass, we saw God's hand in bringing success out of our teammates' work. We also viewed our own ministry as an offshoot of their work. Had it not been for the love and kindness they had poured into the community, it is doubtful that we would have been welcomed with open arms to live and work in Nomba. Had it not been for CSJ, we would not have had a platform from which to begin building relationships, launching our own work in the village. Most importantly, we would not have had the Bible study at which Miséria, Cascão, and Ramos became convicted by the Word of God to follow Jesus Christ. Consequently, the church might not have been established. Our team was dysfunctional, and sometimes things were messy, but God had worked it for good. We held no animosity toward our teammates.

Therefore, we were surprised to learn from *other* missionaries that the Jacksons were planning a visit to Nomba in a few weeks. They had not told us they were coming and it stung to find out the news second hand. That is when we discovered just how great the divide was between us from their point of view. It was strange to me, however, because they had never spoken to us about it. Nobody likes confrontation, but working through conflict is necessary for the sake of relationship, even if it is only to "agree to disagree."

We had not written our last letter to them in haste. We had carefully gone over it several times to make sure there were no personal cutting remarks or sarcasm that might have given offense. Even though the corruption we had warned them about when they were setting up the board of directors had come to pass, we did not say "we told you so" in the letter. We had only stated the facts, as we knew them, and we had given our opinion of what was needed to correct the situation. I pulled the letter back up on my computer and read it again. Had we missed something? Was it too harsh? Had we used the truth like a blunt weapon?

I swallowed my pride and wrote to Holly saying that we had heard they were coming and hoped they would come by for a visit and share a meal with us. I said we were eager to see them and to hear how they were doing, adjusting to life in America. I was careful to say nothing about CSJ or Benne, hoping she would understand we would not have to talk about it unless they wanted to.

Holly wrote back that she was sorry that they hadn't let us know about the visit. She said they would be staying at CSJ and, although their time was short, maybe we could get together. I left her our phone number and told her we were looking forward to seeing them again. That was the last we heard from them. They never called and never stopped by after traveling half way around the world to the same village in Africa. We did not have their phone number. So, to see them, we would have had to track them down at CSJ, which would have been awkward at best. Miséria invited them to come to the Friday night Bible study, where we could have seen them, but they told her they had other plans that night. The Smiths invited them to see their old home and host a dinner for them and us, but they declined the offer. It was plain they did not wish to see us.

I was deeply hurt. I wondered what I had said or done to cause them to feel that way. We had come to Mozambique at their invitation. We had never been included in the major decision-making processes at CSJ, but we had done our best with the situation left to us. We were unwaveringly truthful to them, but we had never said one unkind word. Steve acted as if their rejection of us did not bother him, but I knew it hurt him too.

In their defense, Benne was probably telling them some whopper lies about us. I was told that when Drew went out in the village, Benne was always by his side, staring down anyone who might speak out against his abuses. Even so, we would have thought Drew mature enough to know that only hearing one side of a story is unwise. If he was hearing terrible things about us, why did he not ask us if they were true?

The Jacksons did make time to have dinner with the other missionary family that had served on the board. We were close friends with the Van Steltons. So, sometime later, I asked them if they knew what we might have done to offend the Jacksons. They offered that Holly had spoken about how much of their lives they had poured into CSJ. Maybe it was just too hard, they suggested, to believe that it was not going well. After much introspection, I could not come up with a better explanation, but it did not take away the hurt.

Once again I focused on 1 Corinthians 13 to remember what it means to love. I found the paraphrase in the Message most helpful . . .

> Love never gives up. Love cares for others more than for self . . . [Love] doesn't *force* itself on others . . . [Love] doesn't keep score of the sins of others . . . [Love] puts up with anything, trusts God always, always looks for the best and never looks back.

I made a deliberate decision to forgive the Jacksons, to believe the best of them, and to continue to love them, even if from a distance. I also made the decision to put the whole thing behind me. I would not look back any longer, lest I be paralyzed with self-doubt and useless for the kingdom of God. My resolve would be tested a few months later.

We were Skyping[24] Pete, a close friend from our home congregation, who was also deacon over missions. After a long visit,

---

[24] Skype® is a computer program that allows long distance telephone and video calls to be made through one's computer.

he mentioned in closing something about a letter he had received recently from Drew (who was not a member of our church). We asked him to please expound on the contents of the letter, to which he said, "Oh, you guys don't need to worry about it. I've got you covered."

Apparently, after his return, Drew had sent a letter to our preacher and others in the congregation. The preacher subsequently passed the matter on to Pete to "deal with," since it concerned missions. Pete seemed reluctant to share the letter with us, perhaps fearing he had opened a can of worms. I had to insist, somewhat, that if the letter concerned us, we needed to know what had been said about us. He agreed to forward the letter along with his response.

Even after all that had passed, the contents of the letter shocked me. Drew said that he was "*very* concerned" about our influence in the village and went on to talk about several things that we supposedly had done to harm CSJ. He concluded that we had already "caused enough damage." The things he accused us of, however, were not true.

My opinion of Drew plunged to a new depth. Before I read that letter, I still respected him as a brother in Christ and someone with an earnest heart to do good works for His kingdom. I had been disappointed when he refused to visit us or at least to tell us, face-to-face, what we had done to offend him. Yet this was so much worse. He not only believed the lies Benne had told him about us, but he passed them on to our home congregation.

It was plainly an attempt to get us sent home in disgrace. My guess is that when Benne's attempt to get us kicked out of the country failed, he began a deliberate campaign of slander about us to our teammates, hoping they would do the work for him. Drew had taken the bait. Once he stopped looking for the truth, he opened himself up to delusion. The chief put it this way, "Benne gave Drew strong medicine, so that he would not see the evil that he was doing."

As the chief spoke, he passed his hand over his eyes as if pulling down a veil.

> How great is Your goodness . . . for those
> who take refuge in You . . . You hide them
> in the secret place of Your presence from
> the conspiracies of man; You keep them se-
> cretly in a shelter from the strife of tongues.
> —Psalm 31:19–20

Praise God who protects His children from the lies and slander of the evil one. Pete's letter, in response to Drew's, lacked nothing in Godly wisdom; it was better than any letter we could have written in our own defense. He said they never heard anything more from Drew after that. The whole affair had all happened without our knowledge. Once again, we felt loved and protected by the Father who knows everything and has the power to work it all for our good. We were thankful for faithful friends like Pete who had our back. Keeping my focus on Jesus has enabled me to forgive Drew, to hold no bitterness toward him, and even to pity him.

I hesitated to include this account in our story. The purpose of this book is to glorify our Father, to tell of the wonderful things He has done in our lives, and to encourage others to follow Jesus wherever He may lead them. I wondered if this part of the story would serve that purpose, or was I only including it to vindicate us. Our teammates obviously viewed the situation through a different lens. I am sure there was something we must have said or done at some point that offended them. Maybe it was just a look that was misunderstood. We must have unknowingly given them some cause to believe the lies they heard. We share in the responsibility for the broken relationship between ourselves and our teammates.

In the end, I decided to include this chapter to show how God took care of us and also because sometimes missionaries tend to gloss over the difficult things to the detriment of our work. We want more "workers for the harvest" and we think if we are honest about the bad stuff, others will be afraid to step out in faith. So we don't talk about the bad stuff.

The truth we had learned at MTI in our pre-field training helped us tremendously. The truth is that *most* missionaries do not even complete their first term in the field. Most come home early disillusioned—not from the difficulties of living in a foreign culture—but from disappointment and hurt caused by their own teammates. Because we knew this truth going into the work, we were saddened, but not devastated, when it happened to us.

We tend to hold our teammates to a higher standard. We somehow expect that they will be like-minded, and we will agree on most everything. Once we find out that they are only human, and sometimes hold strong opinions in opposition to our own, the disappointment begins. Much of being a team is learning to work through those differences, embrace those differences, and to respect the diversity of the body of Christ. It requires hard work and maturity, much like a marriage. When there is discord, it takes both sides, determined to work through the problems with respect for the other's point of view, to be successful. It takes truth (both spoken and received in love), and good communication (listening well).

Although it is hard work, the payoff of having a healthy team in the foreign mission field is great. We witnessed this during the time we spent with our other Good News for Africa teammates at our annual retreat. They lived in another province and their team consisted of three families who have worked together for fifteen years now. They are spiritually healthy, their marriages are strong, and their children are happy and well adjusted. The team works together well and plays together well. They are bonded.

When I complemented them on this, they all confessed that it had not been easy. They worked hard to make sure each person on the team felt valued. Not surprisingly, their ministry among the Macua tribe has born a tremendous amount of fruit, and they are still going strong. Even this team, however, had experienced problems early on. There were originally six families. One family returned early due to health problems. Two other families, however, split off into a separate team because of unresolved disagreements. After the team split, the remaining three families were even more diligent to work toward team unity—and God has honored them for their efforts.

The apostle John said it well:

Beloved, if God so loved us, we also ought to love one another . . . We love because He first loved us. If someone says, "I love God," and hates his brother, he is a liar; for the one who does not love his brother whom he has seen, cannot love God whom he has not seen. And this commandment we have from Him, that the one who loves God should love his brother also. —1 John 3:11, 19–21

Part V: Begin Fifth Year in Mozambique and Transition Home, August 2014–April 2015

Chapter 30
Lukia's Suffering

LUKIA'S SUFFERING, AND THAT OF her children, came to a peak in August of 2014. Emilio continued to court the other woman, bringing her food and gifts to the deprivation of his own children. He told Lukia he planned to bring her to live with them. It was more humiliation than Lukia could bear. She told Emilio she would not stand for it any longer, and she went through the traditional methods of reconciliation, asking her eldest brother to reason with him. When he stubbornly refused to budge, her family elders went to his family elders. Eventually, they all went to the chief.

Emilio finally had enough of Lukia's protest. One morning, he threw her and the children out of the home. He even took the unusually cruel step of locking them out of the house, so they could not get any food or clothing. It was especially unjust, because Lukia had worked hard to bring in the corn harvest that year with no help from Emilio. He sent them out with nothing but the clothes on their backs.

It all happened in the predawn hours. Although I awoke to voices raised in argument, I had no idea of the severity of the situation. I did not learn what had happened until later that day, when our guard, Samuel, told me. He said that when the neighbors showed up because of the fighting, Lukia was so ashamed that she ran off on foot with the children to Lumbe, the village of her mother, some fifty kilometers away. He told me that everyone was angry at Emilio for sending them off that way with no food or clothing. He said that his family members had already gone back to the chief. They asked him to convince Emilio to at least let them take their clothes and part of the corn harvest to Lukia, so the children would not starve. Emilio, however, would not even listen to the chief.

Samuel said they would continue to pressure Emilio, because what he was doing was not right in God's eyes. He asked if we would help by taking the supplies to Lumbe in our truck, once they succeeded in convincing Emilio. I told him that we would, of course, help Lukia and the children in any way we could.

I went to Lichinga that day and purchased a change of clothes and a jacket (August is the cold season) for each of the children at the used clothing market. I looked through my own closet and found some items that would fit Lukia. I had been to Lumbe with Lukia only once before, but I knew her family was very poor. So I also packed up some extra corn flour, beans, cooking oil, and soap to help them get by until the family came up with a longer-term solution. I was grieved at the thought of them suffering and also at the loss of their nearness. Lukia had never left before without saying good-bye, so I knew she was hurting deeply.

I drove to Lumbe the next day and found my way to Lukia's mother's hut. They were all happy to see me and recounted the sad story. I asked Lukia where they were staying. She showed me a tiny hut that measured about six feet by eight feet where all five of them were sleeping together. After visiting with Lukia's extended family, I tried to encourage her and the children. I told them what Samuel and the others were doing, and I gave them the items I brought with me. After spending the afternoon together, we prayed. I tried to smile as I said good-bye, but once I was safely out of view, the tears flowed freely.

Several weeks passed before Emilio's family convinced him to relinquish the clothes. They also managed to get a few sacks of corn (less than half the harvest), some of her pots and pans, a blanket, and one chair. It wouldn't be enough to get them through until the next harvest, but it was better than what they had. They loaded the supplies into the pickup, and I drove the family elders to Lumbe.

I thought Lukia would be happy to receive at least these items, but when she saw what we brought, she burst into violent sobs. I put my arm around her and lead her away from the crowd that had gathered. I asked her what was wrong. She explained that by accepting these items, she would be accepting that her marriage was over, and accepting his terms of separation. It wasn't enough, she said. They would not survive until the next harvest.

"I worked so hard in the fields, *Dada*. I brought in the whole harvest by myself. I was a good wife. I never cheated on him. How can he do this to me and his own children? Life is so hard out here. How will we survive?"

It was true. Lumbe was a very poor and remote village. The road to get there was unpaved and decidedly rough. Opportunities to make a living beyond subsistence farming were nonexistent. There was a primary school, but no secondary school for the children, and only one small health post. The people there had suffered much during the war years, many of them fleeing to the

Lichinga district for safety. Those refugees had established the village of Lumbe Dois (Lumbe the Second), where Teresa lived.

"Sister," I told her, "you must be strong for the sake of the children. I know it is hard, but they need you to be strong now. God sees your suffering, and He will provide for you. You will get through this, and life will be better next year after the harvest. I will visit you when I can and help you. I won't forget all the kindness you have shown me. You know that I love you and the children."

Lukia took a deep breath and straightened herself. "I will be strong for the children. We *will* get through this. God will watch over us."

Chapter 31
Preparing for Departure

AUGUST BROUGHT THE CONCLUSION OF our fourth year in Mozambique and the fifth year of our service in the foreign mission field. We had completed our five-year commitment but there were still many loose ends. We applied for the renewal of our visas and simultaneously sought the Lord. We asked friends from our home congregation, CVM, and family members to be in prayer for us. We sought the Lord's direction to know if it was time to come home or if we should commit to another term (each term was two or three years). Not surprisingly, our family was ready for our return but our mentor at CVM wanted us stay in Mozambique. Our church family said they would support us in whichever decision we made.

Although a part of me was ready to go home, I felt it was too early to leave. The Nomba church *elders* were only two years old in the faith. The church had not yet been established a full year. The Smiths had recently moved out of the village to another district. Now a Jehovah's Witness missionary family from Brazil was renting the Jackson's house from CSJ. They had already begun teaching false doctrine to anyone who would listen. I felt like Satan was ready to pounce on the little flock of sheep we would be leaving behind. There were no other missionaries from our church or from Good News for Africa or from CVM coming to continue the work.

Steve, on the other hand, was ready to go home. It wasn't that he thought our work complete, but he was struggling in the culture. We had been in a pressure cooker for the last five years and he was ready to get out. He missed our family. He longed to be a part of our grandchildren's lives while they were still young. We now had five beautiful grandchildren and had not yet met Elliot, the youngest.

If we were to stay a third term, we would be due another three-month furlough in the fall. I encouraged Steve that three months spent with our family would refresh him and give him the strength to continue on one more year for the sake of the fledgling church. That is when he told me, "We need to leave by December, or I'll just be hanging on."

It was clear. It was time to prepare for our departure. When Steve and I began the journey, we had agreed that if either one of us felt they were just "hanging on," it was time to go. We knew our first ministry was to our marriage and to each other. When he used those words, I knew that he was telling me he could not continue. I would not try to convince him to stay any longer. I prayed for the next several weeks that if it was God's will for us to stay longer, He would give Steve both the strength *and* the desire to continue. But if it was His will for us to go home, He would give me peace about leaving.

In time, I received the peace I needed. God reminded me that He was at work before we came, and that His Spirit would continue the work long after our departure. "Yet God is my King of old, working salvation in the midst of the earth" (Psalm 74:12).

It did not depend on us. He had only graciously *allowed* us to participate in His redeeming work. I was overwhelmed with gratitude that He had given us this opportunity to work with Him, for this special flock that had become precious to us.

As if to confirm our decision, we received an email from our renters. They notified us they had been transferred to Houston and would be moving out the first of September. They had been living in our home the entire time we had been serving overseas. We let our friends from church know the situation, and they immediately offered to care for our pets until our return.

We made a plan for our transition and submitted it to the missions committee and also to CVM. We would come home in December and stay three months traveling to supporting churches to report on the work. We would also travel to CVM's home office in Seattle to report there and receive our debriefing. Then we would return to Mozambique in March and April for the first "shuttle mission." We proposed a yearly shuttle mission, or short-term mission trip, with the purpose of encouraging and strengthening the church. We wanted to schedule the first trip before our visas expired to ensure that we would not be denied entry back into Mozambique.

When we broke the news of our impending departure to our loved ones in the church, we had promised that we would be coming back. We wanted to be sure that we would be able to keep our word, at least for the first visit. Both CVM and our home congregation approved our plan. The missions committee was especially glad that we wanted to return each year to strengthen the church.

As our departure date drew near, we continued our work full throttle. Steve was putting up a windmill at the Van Stelton's dairy farm near Mitava village. The windmill was a refurbished Aeromotor from west Texas. It had been donated by an elder of our church, and we had shipped it to Mozambique in our container. We had originally planned to put it at CSJ, but no longer felt that was the best place for it given the circumstances.

We chose to bless the Van Steltons with the windmill because they had a great need for it and they did such wonderful work toward Christ-centered community development. They had a shop in Chiwaula where they sold yogurt made with milk from the farm. Both at the farm and at the shop, they modeled the love of Christ and mentored their employees in the Christian world view. Some of their employees were Christian and the ability to work in a Christian environment was helpful to maturing them in the faith. The Van Steltons were among the first missionaries to the Yao and their commitment to continue to live and work in Mozambique was still very strong.

Steve worked hard to complete the windmill tower with the young men who worked at the farm. The tower would eventually ascend thirty feet high. The work was difficult and dangerous due to the strong winds and the inexperienced crew. All the work had to be done by hand, without heavy equipment or power tools. As always, Steve worked with the young men with a combination of humor, respect, and the love of Christ. He made me proud.

Steve also continued to meet weekly with Cascão. Together they would study the Bible passages in preparation for the Sunday sermons. As I prepared our evening meal on Saturdays, I'd listen to them as Steve patiently went through each verse with Cascão, teaching him to divide the Word carefully. Despite his limited education, Cascão learned quickly. Steve had given him a lengthy list of scriptures that he felt were key to defending the faith. He encouraged Cascão to commit the scriptures to memory over time, so that he would "always be ready to give an answer for the hope he had within him" (1 Pet. 3:15).

When Cascão returned the following week, Steve asked him if he had committed the first scripture to memory yet. Much to our incredulity, he responded that he had committed *all* of them to memory. He then proceeded to recite each scripture, complete with chapter and verse, as we followed along in his Portuguese Bible. Yes, God's Spirit was at work! He had definitely given Cascão a special anointing to lead this church.

Cascão is a humble man from humble beginnings. His father, a Muslim, was a prominent member of the Yao tribe in Lichinga and an advisor to the chief of Chiwaula. He married Cascão's mother, a Nyanga woman and an Anglican, but forbade her to raise their children as Christians.

When Cascão was only six years old, his father became very ill and passed away. His father's family wasted no time in driving his mother out from their home so they could sell it. Homeless and without any means to provide for her children, his mother sent Cascão to live with her brother in Nampula. Cascão's uncle promised that he would provide for him and make sure he received an education. During that time Cascão was exposed to Christianity in the Anglican Church, but he remembered his father's admonition that he should remain a Muslim, and was afraid to leave Islam.

After a few years passed, Cascão's uncle began to neglect him. He did not pay the school fees and consequently, Cascão was expelled from school. His uncle forced him to work as a servant for the family and only gave him leftovers to eat. Hungry and malnourished, Cascão sent a letter to his mother begging her to let him come home. She sold enough produce to travel to Nampula and brought Cascão home to Nomba, where she had settled. She could not afford his school fees but at least he would not go hungry. He went to work in the market carrying bags for tips to supplement the family's income and also helped in the *machamba* that his mother had acquired by that time. He eventually became disillusioned and rejected all religion. He stopped going to mosque and he began to hang out with a group of miscreants he met at the market. Eventually, he got into drugs and alcohol and petty thievery.

Then one summer night in 2012, Cascão had a vision. A strong man dressed in brilliant white pursued him with the intent to kill him. Fearing for his life, Cascão ran as fast as he could away from the man until, at last, he saw him no more. Exhausted, he laid down in the grass and fell asleep. The next morning, he awoke and was about to leave when Benne arrived—Cascão had fallen asleep in Benne's *machamba*. Benne told him he needed some day laborers to work at CSJ. Cascão, still shaken by the vision, agreed to work there.

At lunch that day, Cascão heard the Proclaimer at the Bible study and realized that the man in his vison was trying to kill him because of his sinful lifestyle. He began to study the Bible and ask Jon questions about Jesus. Over the next few months, Jon led Cascão to a saving faith in Jesus Christ, and he was baptized. The change in Cascão was dramatic; everyone in the village noticed it. People were surprised that this former delinquent was now a hardworking, sweet-spirited disciple of Jesus. Some were skeptical at first. They warned us not to let him into our home. Over time the transformation proved to be genuine, however, and even the skeptics had to admit that Cascão was a new man.

A year after his conversion, I invited Cascão to share his testimony with the children in our program. I knew the kids would soon face many of the same challenges and temptations that had led Cascão down the wrong path. Some of them were, no doubt, experiencing the same challenges already. In the Yao culture, it is unusual for a person to admit his sin or weakness. Like many Muslim cultures, it is a shame/honor culture. To confess sin is to be shamed. He bravely bared his soul that day. His repentant heart demonstrated his genuine faith, and I know that his story gave hope to the children.

Just as Steve poured into Cascão, I continued to pour into Miséria. She was the other church "elder" and my child in the faith. Together she and Cascão formed the strong backbone, the core leadership, of the Nomba church. After them, Merina, Julio, and Asainabo provided another layer of leadership. All of them looked to Jon, leader of the Chenganani church, for advice when they needed guidance.

By that time, I had been giving Miséria reading lessons for eighteen months. I had also begun to teach her basic arithmetic. Prior to that time, Miséria never had even one day of schooling. She did not know her letters so we had to start with the alphabet. For each letter, I tried to think of a short Portuguese word beginning with that letter so she would learn the basic concept of phonetics. I wanted to empower her to continue to increase her reading ability long after I was gone.

It was slowgoing at first. I never realized how much I took for granted the conceptual link that each letter has its own sound or sounds depending on where it was placed in the word. Added to that, we were both working in our second language. Even though she had lacked opportunities to study as a child, Miséria is very intelligent. Furthermore, she proved to be the most driven student I had ever taught. The only other students I had taught were veterinary students during my residency program at the University of Pennsylvania. Professional students at an Ivy League School are extremely driven, but Miséria's drive surpassed even theirs! She was determined to learn to read the Bible so she could teach others the Word of God. To that end, we began each session in prayer, confident that God keeps His promises.

I gave her a notebook that I would fill with short sentences for her to practice at home. I found I had to change the sentences every week because she would memorize them quickly. It was sometimes hard to determine if she was really reading or just reciting the lines from memory. It was challenging at times, but I found that teaching her to read was the most rewarding thing I had done in Mozambique, second only to introducing her to Jesus.

Teaching her arithmetic was much easier. She already knew how to do it in her head. Since she was a child she had been practicing each time she went to the market. So that is where we began. I introduced word problems with piles of beans and nuts, as if we were shopping. Then it was only a matter of teaching her how to translate those word problems into a numerical equation. Next, I taught her the rules for solving the numerical equation. When the equations contained only single and double digits, it was difficult for her to see the value of following the rules rather than doing the arithmetic in her head. Once we advanced to triple digits, however, she realized the importance of following the rules. She delighted in the fact that she could solve any problem, no matter how big the numbers were.

By the time we were ready to leave, Miséria was reading her Bible. I remember well the first time she read to us. She was sitting at our kitchen table and we had just presented the Bible to her as a gift. I prayed that the reading level would not be so difficult as to discourage her. Overjoyed to at last have her own Bible, she opened it to the passage I had marked. The passage was Mathew 22:36–40, regarding the greatest commandment. She read slowly and carefully, sounding out each syllable with great concentration. As we looked on in amazement, Steve and I both cried silent tears of joy.

Even though she worked long days at CSJ during the week and at her *machamba* on the weekends, Miséria practiced reading every night. She told me that she would fall asleep while reading, and that she slept with her Bible by her side. If she woke up during the night, she would read some more using the headlight I had given her.

I also taught Miséria to write. Writing was harder for her. She was still struggling to figure out how to spell the words she wished to write, but I encouraged her to continue to practice. I wanted her to have the freedom to express her thoughts in writing. So I gave her another notebook and her homework each week was to write me a letter. I asked her to continue to write me letters each week while we were gone. I would look forward to reading them when we returned in March. She promised she would write me every week.

In addition to our work with the church, we were also working on getting a borehole for our neighbors. On the opposite side of the village, the water table was higher. Each family had a hand-dug well from which they could draw water. On our side of the village, however, the granite slab and the depth of the water table made that impossible. The only source of water easily accessible to our neighbors was a spring that was reduced to a mere mud puddle by the end of the dry season. Cholera outbreaks occurred yearly. Although we allowed our neighbors to get their drinking water from our well, it did not produce sufficient water for other uses. Additionally, because it was over sixty meters deep, it required a submersible pump, a generator to run the pump, and fuel to run the generator. The more sustainable option of a hand pump only worked on wells up to forty-five meters deep.

We formed a "water committee" of men we trusted and one woman who was an elderly matriarch. It was important to have at least one woman who was not afraid to stand up to the men to communicate the need for repairs. Because hauling water was work the women did, if the pump broke the men might see it as the women's problem. There were no Christians yet on our side of the village. So we chose Muslim men we knew had a good work ethic and desire to do well. We also selected men from different families so as not to give any one family too much power. Steve had already worked with some of the men to repair existing government wells in the village. Consequently, they knew some of the basic things to look for and where to buy parts in Lichinga.

The committee would also be responsible for collecting a small monthly fee from each family using the well. The collected funds were to be safeguarded and later used to buy parts for repairs. We asked the committee members to meet with the villagers and choose three possible sites for the new well that would be centrally located, accessible to all. The final site would be determined by the well driller's opinion of where the most abundant supply of water was located.

Unfortunately, there was only one well driller in the entire region with the equipment to get through the granite. He was a Muslim man named Aslam who lived in Lichinga but traveled frequently throughout the province contracting wells for the government and businesses. He was a very busy man and difficult to reach. After nearly six months of trying to get him to come out and give us a quote without success, we were afraid we'd never get the well in before it was time to go.

Exasperated, I relayed our difficulties to another missionary one day. Tyren and Tiffany lived on the opposite side of Lichinga. We did not see them often but they were a delightful couple from Connecticut with four lovely children. I usually ran into Ty on those rare occasions that I went shopping at central market in Lichinga. He always had a couple of street kids by his side, holding his hand. Although I could count the number of times I ran into him on one hand, each encounter made a profound impact on me in some way.

The year before, we were at central market when Tyren told me about the attack on his family. He recounted a horrifying story of a gang of men armed with machetes, iron bars, and an axe, who assaulted them at home one night. Ty was outside when they arrived and the attackers mistook him, being African-American, for the guard. They beat him mercilessly with an iron bar. When one of them raised an axe, poised to come down on Ty's head, all he could say was "Oh Lord, not the axe!" The assailant's arm froze in midair and he could not complete the fatal blow. Ty went on to testify about how Jesus worked that night to protect him and his family through the ordeal. He gave God the glory and I was left humbled by their ability to praise God amid such an extreme trial. I don't think they even considered going home because of it. If Steve and I had endured such an assault we probably would have returned to the States quickly and permanently. Our faith was not that strong. But "iron sharpens iron" and just hearing of their faith and commitment bolstered our own.

When Tyren heard about our difficulties reaching Aslam, he offered to try and get in touch with him for us. Ty had a good relationship with Aslam, who had put in their well a few years previously. He knew Aslam had been out of town on a job but said he would talk to him once he returned.

Shortly before our departure, Aslam came out to meet us and give us a quote. He gave us a very reasonable quote because we were "friends of Tyren" and "he said you want to help the people." He also guaranteed the well would have a sufficient supply of water or we would owe nothing. Unfortunately, however, he would not be able to drill the well until he returned from another journey. He needed to travel to South Africa and purchase some supplies. We asked him if he needed a deposit since we would be leaving the country before he could begin the work. That is when he shocked us by saying, "You don't need to pay anything up front. Because you are Tyren's friend, I trust you. I will put in a good well for you."

That was the effect Ty had on people; he had that rare, sweet Spirit of Christ.

Chapter 32
Saying Good-bye

THE LAST SATURDAY BEFORE OUR departure, we went to the chief's house to say our good-byes to him and his wife. He told us we did not have to worry; our house would be secure, and ready for our return. His wife brought out a big bag of beans and a guinea hen for me to take back to our family as a gift. I thanked her for the beans but told her they would not let me bring the hen into the country. I would be sure to tell our family, however, how much she wished to bless them.

The last Sunday came way too soon for me. I loved worshiping with "the Love of Jesus" church. For our final year in Mozambique, at last, we had the love and fellowship of a body of believers with whom we could worship. I took in every moment of that last Sunday like cool water on a hot summer day. My emotions kept welling up each time I met eyes with another.

I watched the children singing, so many I had known for years. What would their future hold? It seemed brighter now than when we first came. Julio, their teacher, had recently married a beautiful woman from Beira named Eugenia. She was from a different tribe and was also from the city, accustomed to a finer lifestyle than Julio was able to provide. The marriage had gotten off to a rocky start. Would they make it? I prayed that they would learn to love and respect one another.

I looked over at Cascão and Merina. Baby Felizado (Happiness) was strapped to Merina's back and two-year-old Esperança (Hope) was tugging on her mother's hand. Merina's smile was radiant as she sang and danced before the Lord with Felizado going along for the ride. Before she knew Jesus, Merina had a shy and solemn personality. But He had transformed her very nature to one that was effervescent, bubbling over with joy. I prayed that God would continue to bless this family with a strong and loving marriage. I prayed that He would protect them from the evil one, who seeks to destroy marriages, to destroy families, and to destroy the church.

I was sandwiched between Miséria and Asainabo. They both sang beautiful harmony, and when I sat between them, I could sing too. I loved these two ladies. To keep from crying, I had to tell myself we were just going on furlough—it wasn't time to say our final good-byes yet.

Cascão and Steve preached a wonderful message together. At the end of the service, Cascão asked us to sit in the center of the circle. Everyone gathered around us and began to pray over us. Some were praying in Chiyao. Others prayed in Portuguese. They laid their hands gently on us, and prayed fervently over us. I felt Miséria's tears falling on my shoulder. I felt my own hot tears streaming down my cheeks. Assainabo wailed out loud. Even the men were crying as they prayed.

After the prayer, we gave hugs and kisses and said good-bye to the ones we would not see again for several months. I knew Miséria and Cascão would be coming with us to the airport, so I refused to say good-bye to them yet.

I couldn't eat much lunch. I needed a break from my own overwhelming emotions, so I took a walk alone in the bush. The lush grass, almost waist high, waved gently in the breeze, and the path cut narrowly through it. It gave me the sensation that I was wading in the ocean. For a fleeting moment, as I looked across the familiar valley, I felt as if I was in another dimension. I was walking through eternity. God seemed very near in that moment. I descended the steep hillside taking in the fresh air. It felt good to be able to breathe deeply without crying. I crossed the creek at the bottom of the valley and then began ascending the next hill when I heard a familiar voice calling, *"Dada!"*

I looked east across the valley to a distant hill, but I couldn't see well enough to identify the caller. "Lukia, is that you?" I shouted.

"Of course it's me, can't you see me? Wait there, I'm coming over!"

Like a graceful deer, she lit down the hillside, crossed the valley, jumped the creek, and was at my side. After we embraced, we faced each other, holding hands.

"Lukia! It is so good to see you. You know we are leaving Tuesday. We will be gone several months, but we will come back in March. I'm so glad God brought us together. I did not want to leave without saying good-bye. But you were gone when I went to Lumbe and I didn't know where to find you."

"Sister, life has been hard. I'm moving back to Nomba with the children when I'm done planting my *machamba*. That is where I have been. My sister and brother-in-law have a house in Nomba. They are going to let us borrow a small hut on their property, so the children can continue to go to school in Nomba."

"That is wonderful news, but how will I know how to find you when I return?" I asked.

"Bwana and Judit will watch for you. When they hear you are back, we will come and bring you to our house. Besides, it is not too far from Miséria's house. We will be studying the Bible again on Friday nights, so we will know when you are back."

I was so happy to hear this and to have the chance to say good-bye to my dear friend. We prayed together once more. I invited her to come back to the house with me, but she said it wasn't safe because Emilio might see her. He wanted her dead and had paid the witch doctor to put a curse on her.

We hugged and said good-bye. As I walked back home, the sadness and tears I was trying to escape found me again. My dearest friend still did not know Jesus as Lord and Savior. She was going through the worst trial of her life without the knowledge of His love. I had told her about Him, but had I said enough? Had I done enough? Had I prayed enough? I resolved to pray more.

When I got to the top of the last hill, I looked back one last time and prayed over the valley. I prayed for the people who farmed the land. I prayed for a good harvest. I claimed the valley for Jesus as I had done so many times before. The sun was setting to the west casting long shadows. I knew I needed to get home, but I lingered just a little while longer. I love the soft pink light and changing hues of dusk. I tried to capture the light, the gentle breeze, and the lush green valley and sear them into my memory. I took a deep breath and caught the familiar smell of smoke coming from the village as the women began preparing the evening meal. After taking one last look, I headed back home.

The next day was a blur. I am sure I spent it packing but I don't remember much. In the afternoon I went to Guida's house and sat with her and the children. I reminded them how much God loved them. I told them they must never forget that. I told them how much I loved them. I would pray for them, and I would not forget them.

Melody hugged me tightly with tears in her eyes. I had only recently discovered that this bright child could not read, not even simple words. She was in the fifth grade and a good student. I knew Melody was capable of learning to read but the school system had failed her. There wasn't enough time to teach her myself, so I had asked Julio to give her private lessons until she could read. He promised me he would. I looked at Melody and told her that whatever she learned from Julio, she needed to teach it to her younger siblings. In that way, they would all learn to read. She nodded her head and said, "I promise, *Tia*. I'm going to learn to read, and then I'm going to teach them. I want to be a teacher like Julio."

Our plane left the next morning. Cascão and Miséria waited with us in the airport until they called us to the boarding area. By that time I had cried out all my tears and was emotionally drained. Steve and I hugged them one last time.

"Don't forget to write me every week," I said with a smile. "I can't wait to read your letters!"

Miséria replied, "I won't forget, Mamãe, I will pray for you every day, so you will come back to us."

"Thank you," I said. "I will pray for you as well. It won't be long—you will see—we'll be back. Please don't be sad. We'll be back soon. Remember how much God loves you, and I love you too."

Steve and I boarded the plane and began our journey home. It really did not feel like good-bye yet. I knew the next few months would pass quickly, and we would be back. The hard good-byes would come in April.

Chapter 33
Coming Home

OUR FLIGHT HOME HAD A connection in Johannesburg, South Africa. We felt we needed some time to decompress before going home. So we decided to take a few days to see Capetown (using our own funds) before flying on to the United States. We had heard from our missionary friends that Capetown was a wonderful city. We found it to be just that—quaint yet bursting with life.

We took a tour of the city and of the historic vineyards in the rolling green hills outside of the city. One of the vineyards, Groot Constancia, had been established by the Dutch in the 1600s. Napoleon had purchased the entire vintage one year. The tour that impacted us the most, however, was a boat ride to Robben Island. It was there that Nelson Mandela spent the better part of three decades of his life in prison. The prison had been turned into a museum and our tour guide had also been a political prisoner during the turbulent final decade of the apartheid years.

We saw the tiny cell that housed Mandela when he was in solitary confinement. We also saw the larger group cell. We saw the limestone quarry where the prisoners, including Mandela, did hard labor. We learned that even within the prison, apartheid rules separated the prisoners based on ethnicity. "Colored" men (Indian or mixed race) got better food rations and clothing than the black men. The black men were issued shorts instead of trousers because they were considered boys, not men. One of Mandela's first victories in prison was getting that rule changed.

After visiting Robben Island, my interest was piqued and I purchased Mandela's autobiography *Long Walk to Freedom*. I began reading it on our flight home. I was captivated by the narrative. The book is a treasure not only for the history of a truly great leader, but it also captures the essence of Africa in its pages. I have great respect for this man who was able to extend grace for the sake of his country, after so much of his life had been stolen away. His life is an inspiring story of how one man's selfless leadership coupled with the forgiveness and cooperation of many saved an entire country from the brink of chaos, violence, and destruction. What a contrast he was to the divisive and corrupt leaders who stoke the flames of bitterness for political advantage. South Africans of all colors will tell you that Mandela saved their country from destruction. He chose the path of peace over the way of vengeance. In doing so, he kept South Africa from tearing apart at the seams during that time of momentous upheaval.

We returned to Johanneesburg and flew out the next evening. Our fifteen-hour transatlantic flight ended in Atlanta—almost home. Neither of us ever sleeps much on the transatlantic, and we are invariably in a terrible daze by the time the plane lands. Despite that, when we get back on American soil, there is always a sense of relief. We can drink out of the water fountains, and the food is safe to eat. If we don't make the connecting flight, finding a hotel is not a big deal. We don't need to exchange currency; we just use the debit card. The bathrooms all have soap and toilet paper, and the toilets flush. We can speak English. We get to the immigration desk and know they will stamp our passports and let us pass. They even say: "Welcome back to America." We are home.

After the usual routine of immigration, we went through customs where they discovered the beans the chief's wife had given me. Steve didn't have to say a word. He looked at me and I knew what he was thinking, *You just had to bring those beans!*

We were directed to load all our bags back on the cart and go through an agriculture inspection station. Once there we had to unload them again so they could be inspected. The officer was a large black man who carefully went through our bags to see if we had any other plant products. When he didn't find any, he took the beans.

I spoke up. "You can't take the beans! They were a gift."

Again, Steve looked at me.

"Oh, don't worry, I won't keep your beans," the man said. "I am just going to clean them to get out any foreign material."

With that, he emptied the sack into a sifter and began cleaning the beans. Shake, shake, toss, shake, shake, toss. It was the familiar rhythm the ladies in the village used to remove rocks from their beans. Shake, shake, toss, shake, shake, toss. The man clearly knew how to sift beans. He did not have a noticeable accent, but I said, "You are from Africa, I can tell by the way you clean those beans."

He laughed and confessed that he was, indeed, from Nigeria and had been cleaning beans since he was a child. He was done in no time and we were on our way to catch our connecting flight to Austin. I was rather pleased that my beans were clean; nothing is worse than biting down on a rock. Steve, however, was still aggravated about all the extra loading and unloading he had to do because of those beans.

"I had to bring them," I explained. "When we go back in March, she is going to ask me if my family liked her beans. I can't *lie* to her."

Steve replied, "Never again."

After our final flight, Mom and Dad met us at the airport in Austin. We looked rough but they looked great. They would soon be turning eighty years old but were both active and blessed with good health. They looked and acted ten years younger than most people their age. It was wonderful to see them again.

After spending a week with Mom and Dad catching up on all the news, eating beans, and getting over jet lag from crossing seven times zones, it was time to move on. Steve and I made the six-hour drive back to our home in northeast Texas. We were a little apprehensive about what our home would look like after over three months of vacancy. We knew we would have a lot of work to do cleaning the place up. Even so, we were eager to be home again.

As we drove up our long driveway (it is about 1/3 of a mile), we were amazed that the pastures were mowed. We got to the house, and all our dearest friends from church were there waiting for us. What a beautiful surprise! We were overwhelmed. They had been caring for our dog and horses for the past three months. As if that were not enough, they had spent the last week cleaning our house top to bottom, mowing the yard and even brush hogging the pasture. Later we found out they had also mended fences and repaired the tractor. We felt so loved by this special group of friends that had been our prayer warriors the entire time we were overseas—our dear brothers and sisters in Christ.

We were finally home.

Chapter 34
Reporting and Readjusting to America

WE SPENT OUR FIRST FEW weeks reconnecting with friends and family. I went to my continuing education meeting where I had the chance to share about the work in Mozambique at an evening seminar that CVM hosted. Then it was Christmas with our children and grandchildren in southeast Oklahoma, more relatives in central Oklahoma, and back down to central Texas for New Year's with my side of the family.

After spending a week at home, we were off again to Seattle to meet with the CVM home office staff. There were more speaking engagements and we received our debriefing, evaluation, and counseling. *Whew!* Thankfully, we were deemed sound of mind, emotionally stable, and spiritually healthy. We were grateful for all the training, encouragement, support, and prayers we had received from the people at CVM through the years. We discussed our options for continuing our relationship with them and decided to transition to associate status when our current term ended. Associate status was a good fit for us because we would still be able to raise funds for the work and have the oversite and accountability that CVM offered. The only difference between associate and full-time field workers was we would no longer use any funds for our personal living expenses. Rather, it would all be used for the project and travel back and forth. After a good time of fellowship, we flew back to Texas.

Finally, we could enjoy being back home, sleeping in our own bed, for a few weeks before returning to Mozambique. I helped Steve update his resume and he wasted no time beginning a job search. We were also doing some much needed repairs on our home and around the farm. It seemed our expectations of what we could achieve each day were very high now that we were back in America.

One morning Steve and I were arguing over some minor thing about the house and he began to have chest pains. I rushed him to the ER because he has a family history of heart disease, so we took it seriously. His blood pressure was sky high but, thankfully, no signs of a heart attack or blockage. They kept him in the hospital overnight and put him on medication to control his blood pressure. We were thankful it happened in America. Had we been in Mozambique, it would have meant an emergency flight to South Africa to get proper care. It was a wakeup call for both of us to relax, to take time to exercise, and to get our expectations back in line with reality.

I called the church leaders and other friends in Mozambique every week. We were thrilled to learn that Mariamo and three other new believers had been baptized shortly after we left. We were especially excited because none of them had been evangelized directly by us. It had been through the efforts of the church leaders in Nomba and Chenganani. They were our first spiritual grandchildren, so to speak. It gave us reassurance that, through His Spirit, the church would continue to grow and multiply amongst the Yao despite persecution, just as it has been doing in Muslim people groups worldwide.

It wasn't long before we were packing again for our first shuttle trip to Mozambique. Our bags were full of Proclaimers, Portuguese Bibles, and water filters. We would stay a full month this first trip. We knew that on future trips we probably wouldn't have enough vacation time to stay that long, but we were glad we could this time. Our friends, Brenda and Lanny, were going to join us for the last two weeks. It would be their second trip to Mozambique. They had also come in 2011 and encouraged us in the work. I think they sensed the tremendous emotional upheaval we were about to go through and just wanted to help us walk through it. We were glad they were coming as they always knew how to make us laugh when things got too heavy. They were good sports and let us fill their bags with Proclaimers and Bibles as well. On the trip home, we would fill their bags with our personal belongings.

Chapter 35
The End of a Beautiful Season

OUR THREE-DAY JOURNEY BACK TO Mozambique was tiring but uneventful. When we finally arrived at the village we were warmly greeted by our neighbors and church family. Cascão, Merina, and Miséria had stocked our pantry full of corn flour, rice, beans, sweet potatoes, onions, garlic, tomatoes, peppers, cooking oil, and salt—foodstuffs typically consumed by Mozambicans. Beyond that, however, they had also gone to Lichinga and purchased imported *Arungu* food like eggs, powdered milk, canned tuna, spaghetti, ketchup, mayonnaise, and cookies for us to enjoy. And our vegetable garden was full of lettuce and greens ready to harvest when needed.

They had also prepared a lovely dinner for us: xima, rice, beans, greens, chicken, and a giant salad. We wondered if little Esperança, Cascão and Merina's daughter, would be shy since we had been gone so long, but after dinner she crawled up into Steve's lap and fell right to sleep. After sharing dinner with us and catching up on the latest news, our guests left us to settle in.

Over the next four weeks, we had a constant stream of visitors to our home. The chief and his wife both came with their youngest children. As I predicted, they were eager to know if our family liked the beans from their *machamba*. I was so glad that I could *truthfully* tell her how much we had enjoyed them.

Teresa, Lucia, and many others I had treated were also among the visitors. They all brought gifts of produce from their garden to say thank you and welcome us home. Teresa had remarried and had a beautiful baby girl named Dominga (the feminine version of Domingo, which means *Sunday*). Lucia was happily living back in Nomba now with her husband and two children.

One day, Frankie, the man who mixed concrete to build our house, came to visit. We had not seen him since the day we prayed for him to find a better job two years prior. We were delighted to learn that not long after we prayed, he had been accepted to train as a policeman in Maputo. He said it was rigorous training but he passed the course and was then assigned to the immigration office in Lichinga. Frankie had come to thank us for praying for him. We were happy he had landed a secure job with good pay so he could support his family. But we were also concerned about his spiritual welfare. He was coming in at a low-level position to a department that was totally corrupt. We prayed with him once again—that he would not be overcome by evil, but would overcome evil with good.

True to her word, it wasn't long before Lukia arrived with Bwana, Judit, Aida, and Judah. After our visit, I gave them a ride home so I could learn where they were staying. It was a small hut on the opposite side of the village, about a half mile from Miséria's house. Although it wasn't ideal for them to be living in a borrowed house, I was glad they were back in Nomba. Now the children could continue in school with their old friends and they would receive spiritual nourishment at the Friday night Bible studies. I gave Lukia one of the Proclaimers we brought with us and she promised to listen to it with the children and her sister's family every night.

Lukia was desperately trying to make ends meet until the harvest. It had been a very difficult year for the family. She never asked me for help, but I knew she needed it. So I took her to Lichinga one day and purchased a five-gallon bucket of cooking oil, a twenty-kilogram sack of rice, and a carton of soap for her to set up a small business outside of their home. Such items were not readily available in the village, so could be sold at a markup. I gave her all my plastic bottles and glass jars I had saved. She divided up the oil and cut up the bars of soap and resold them. She sold the rice by the cup. By the next time I came to visit her she had already used some of her profits to purchase dried fish to add to her wares.

I had told Miséria I wanted her to come over on Thursday nights, as she had done before, to practice her reading. Miséria's reading level had continued to improve. She presented me with the notebook full of the letters she had written each week. It is my most treasured keepsake from Mozambique. Her heart was, and still is, so full of love that she was constantly sharing Christ wherever she went. Even if it meant abuse, she just could not help herself. Her greatest desire was for all of her of children and grandchildren to know Jesus, so that is what we prayed for most often.

On Friday nights, we went to the Bible study at Miséria's home. Cascão and Merina were always there with Esperança and Felizado. Although Miséria hosted the study, Cascão led it. He had a broader knowledge of scripture having been to the Disciple Training School followed by two years of private study with Steve. Many people were attending that study including Mariamo with her youngest daughter Eva, and Lukia with her children. Esperança always went straight to her Uncle Steve, but Aida and baby Judah wanted to sit in my lap.

Mariamo had grown even more in her understanding and passion for God's word. It was plain that she possessed the Holy Spirit. She had endured much persecution from her mother and brothers because of her decision to follow Jesus and be baptized, but she persevered. Like Miséria she had a heart to share Jesus, and the two of them frequently worked together to do just that. Eva had become close to Miséria and her youngest son Bonifacio. Because of the hostilities at home, she spent more time at Miséria's house than her own.

People of the village knew that God was "with Miséria" and they would frequently approach her for prayers for healing. She would pray for them and tell them to come back on Friday so the whole group could pray for them. It was quite a ministry. Even though many were healed, the women only came at night. They were fearful their families would punish them if they found out they were seeking help from the Christians.

We always began and ended the study with prayers and sometimes with a song of praise. The women and children who had slipped in quietly during the study, sat some distance away from the circle. They waited respectfully until the end of the study when Miséria would present them to the rest of the group. Then they would sit in the center and we would pray over them for healing and for them to know Jesus as Lord. Much of the growth of the church over the next two years would come from seekers who had joined this group.

The Wednesday night group was never as strong and had floundered during our absence. Guida had married a man from Malawi and for some reason was distancing herself from the church. She would not present him to us. It seemed there was something she was ashamed of. She told me that he was a policeman and was frequently out of town. I suspect that maybe he had taken her as a second wife, because they never had a public ceremony, he just moved in with her. Polygamy is common in African society, regardless of religion. Guida knew it was wrong to marry a man that already had a wife.

I think she was afraid that since we were leaving she would not be able to support her large family as a single mother. I could not blame her; I had never been in her position. I had a long talk with her about it. We had been planning to give her a sum of money large enough to get her started in a business from home. We still did that even though she had married, but it hurt to think that she married out of desperation instead of love.

I was also concerned for Melody and Vania; they were beautiful girls. Would they be safe with this man? Melody had been in the children's program for four years. We taught the girls to stand up for themselves and say "no" to men asking for sexual favors, even if it was a teacher or another authority figure. It was common for girls in secondary school to be told they would not pass the class unless they had sex with their teacher or school administrator. The following year, these same girls would have to drop out of school altogether to take care of their infant.

There was nothing more I could do about the situation but to pray and encourage Guida to come back into fellowship with the church. I told her they would welcome her in and give her the encouragement she needed to stay strong in the Lord. When I told her how much I loved and cared for her, she broke down in tears, but she still would not reveal her heart. I put my arm around her and tried to comfort her. Something was terribly wrong. I asked her to let the children continue to go to church even if she could not bring herself to go, and she agreed. It gave me some comfort, but I still grieved for Guida. Marriage was supposed to be joyful, but she had no joy, only sorrow.

Between all the visiting, we had many preparations to make before our departure. We would not return for an entire year, maybe longer. We had considered selling or renting our home, but we wanted to be able to stay there during our future visits. There was no other suitable place to stay in the village, especially if we were to bring a team.

We decided to give our home and the land surrounding it to the church. After what happened with CSJ, we did not want to give it immediately, however, until the church leadership proved to be worthy stewards. We told them they could use our home and property for ministry in our absence. We eventually planned to give it to them outright but thought it best to do it gradually so no one would be tempted to privatize it.

For the sake of our guards, we decided not to keep the solar panel system. It was valuable enough to attract professional gangs with firearms, and we did not want to needlessly put their lives in danger. We knew how to live without electricity and could certainly manage for a few weeks at a time on our return trips. We decided to give our solar panel system to the Smith family. They were living in an outlying district where the hope of getting electricity in the coming years was slim. They also had a large family and did not have enough funding to buy a good system. It seemed to us to be good stewardship of Kingdom resources to bless them in this way—we had freely received this blessing and we would freely give it back to the Lord. They were overwhelmed with gratitude because they had been praying for resources to buy a good system.

It was tempting to leave the truck with the church. It would help them and allow us to have transportation when we returned. The problem was that no one in the church had a license to drive and the process of getting a driver's license for a Mozambican usually required a bribe. There was a school of driving in Lichinga. We already knew of several men, however, who had sacrificed to pay for the course, only to complete the course and be told they would not be issued a license unless they also paid the bribe. We wanted no part of that.

Instead, we put the truck up for sale and it was quickly purchased by another missionary family whose current vehicle was spent. We put the funds we received for the truck back into the project account we kept through CVM. It was to be used for the children's ministry of the church and future trips back to Mozambique. We locked Steve's motorcycle up in the shipping container along with our bicycles. They would serve as our transportation on future trips if we could not borrow a car.

It was important for me to find a good home for Nando. Guida's family had always cared for him before when we were gone, but I was afraid he would get stolen if we left him with her. Big dogs were used to guard the *machambas* from thieves and wild animals, but they were treated harshly. They were kept tied up to keep them from running away, which made them easy prey for hyenas. It was a fate I could not bear to think of for Nando. I briefly considered bringing him back to the States, but that would have been so hard on him. It would entail four flights over two days and then a month of quarantine. He was a gentle dog, but had an aggressive streak. I feared the trauma of bringing him to America would turn him into an aggressive dog.

Thankfully, another missionary family from South Africa agreed to take him. Alfred and Belinda Paetzold lived in an outlying district where they were beginning a new work amongst the Yao. They had three athletic sons who spent hours on bush walks, and I knew Nando would be happy with them. There was nothing Nando liked better than going on bush walks. Belinda had asked me if she could purchase our couch when we left. Remember that lumpy sleeper sofa? It did not look like much in America, but it looked great in Africa, especially to a family of five who did not have a couch. I told her we would give them the couch as a "thank you" for providing Nando with a good home. We could manage without the couch when we returned.

We had hoped we could get Aslam out that month to drill the well, but we received some unfortunate news. While he was in South Africa, international tensions had increased between Mozambican immigrants looking for work and unemployed South Africans. Outbreaks of violence and rioting had occurred and the press dubbed the problem "xenophobia." To quell the violence, the two countries had temporarily shut down the border crossing between them, and Aslam was unable to return to Mozambique with his supplies. We knew the situation was temporary, however, and continued to have peace that the borehole would eventually get drilled.

A few days before our departure date, Tyren and Tiffany came to see us. They wanted to pray a blessing over us. It is strange, but praying with them is the last thing I remember on that trip. I know our last week had many sweet times of worship, fellowship, and saying good-bye to our church family as well as our loved ones who still did not know Christ. But while I remember so much of what I have written so far like it happened yesterday, I cannot remember saying those final good-byes. There is a gap—I think it just hurt too much. The next thing I remember was Steve and Lanny and Brenda waiting in the car, motor running, saying, "Julie, we have to go now or we are going to miss our flight."

I was telling our guards and Miséria good-bye. I was also exhorting them to listen to the Proclaimer and remember that God loves them. Miséria wanted to go with us to the airport but there just wasn't room with four people and the luggage. The next thing I remember is staring out the window of the plane at the lush green hills below and crying. My sadness was profound and the tears flowed freely. Part of my sadness was leaving the people we loved. My heart was torn, and a part of my heart would stay forever with them.

As I looked down on the land that I had grown to love, it dawned on me that it hurt deeply because I had loved well. I had not held anything back. I had not guarded my heart. As our time together drew to an end, I did not protect myself by pulling back. I loved them to the end. I don't think it is possible to love like that unless it comes from Jesus. I knew that He had loved them through us. Likewise, we had received His love through them. The love of Jesus is unconditional and the only love that truly satisfies.

Another part of my sadness came from the realization that a beautiful season of our life had come to an end. We would serve God wherever we lived and in whatever occupation, but it wouldn't be quite like this. God had affirmed us over and over again on this journey. From the beginning to the end, I had never doubted that we were in His perfect will. I knew we were doing that good work that He had prepared specifically for us to walk in (Eph. 2:10). Would we find the next good work? Would we continue to have that assurance?

Some things God can only teach us when we are on our knees and there is no better way to keep us in that position than to call us to serve Him in our weakness. I think that is why He tells us to "Go!" He wants to get us out of our comfort zone to where we *must* rely on Him. Only then can He mold and shape us into useful instruments through which He can transmit His love through the power of the Holy Spirit. Only then will the glory be His alone.

Dear Reader,

I hope that the story of our journey will encourage you to examine your own calling. How is God calling you to participate in the Great Commission (Matt. 28:19–20)? Are you being called to support missionaries through prayers, finances, or logistical help? Or is He calling you to be a "goer"? Whichever way He is calling you today, don't be surprised if tomorrow you hear a different call. As God's children, we must hold on to our dreams loosely, leaving room for Him to work.

Spend quiet time alone with Him. Tune your ear to Him. Strain to hear the Shepherd's voice and when you hear it, trust Him! Should you discover that He is calling you in your weakness to *go*, don't be afraid to walk by faith. Follow Him wherever He leads you, and you will find Him there. His strength is sufficient for the task and you will grow in faith and knowledge of Him. Better still, you will grow in His perfect love. It is a privilege you will never regret. That is a promise.

Epilogue
Since Then

- True to his word, Aslam came in July of 2015 and drilled an excellent well with an abundant supply of clean water. The chief and all our neighbors came to the dedication of the well. Cascão read the story of Jesus at the well (John 4) which led to a lively discussion about what Jesus meant when He spoke of "Living Water." They discussed how our souls need this living water just as our bodies need physical water. Several people decided to join a Bible study to learn more.

- The church literally loved Lukia to Christ. They used their collected offerings to help her build a small house she could call her own on a plot of land close to the church. She and the children would no longer have to fear being homeless again. They helped her to get through the most difficult time of her life. She gave her life to Christ and was baptized in August 2015. Four other believers were baptized that same day in the crocodile-infested waters.

- Mariamo became ill in September 2015 and was hospitalized for pneumonia. Church leaders visited her daily and prayed over her, but her health continued to deteriorate until she passed away two weeks later. The doctors said she had a chronic lung condition from selling pesticides for many years without protection. We suspect it was either lung cancer or fibrotic lung disease. To the end, however, she kept the faith and proclaimed Christ as her Savior, eagerly reaching out to others with the Good News. From the time we first met her, Mariamo had a weak and raspy voice. I wonder if she knew her time on earth was short. I am thankful she had the opportunity to hear the gospel and believe.

Mariamo's mother blamed the church for her daughter's death. She said it was their prayers that took her life. She made Eva return her mother's Bible and Proclaimer to Miséria. Eva was heartbroken both for the loss of her mother and the Word of God that she loved to hear. Miséria had to avoid going anywhere near the mother's house because she had threatened to kill her. But Eva would sneak over to Miséria's house and, eventually, Miséria took her in as her own. Almost a year had passed when Mariamo's mother came to visit Miséria one day and said, "Why don't you ever come by to see me anymore?"

"Because you said you would *kill* me," Miséria reminded her gently.

She told Miséria that she was not angry anymore, and she wanted to study the Bible with her. She wanted to learn more about the Jesus her daughter so loved.

- Tyren gave the ultimate gift of his life while serving in Mozambique. He passed away on December 19, 2015 after suffering from malaria, leaving behind Tiffany and their four children. When Tyren got sick, he was preparing a Christmas celebration for the inmates of the local prison. The prisons are, no doubt, some of the darkest places in Mozambique. Tyren was working there to bring the light of Christ and the hope of salvation. If you go to prison in Mozambique, you don't receive much food unless someone from the outside brings it to you. The feast Tyren was preparing for them included chicken, a luxury for the average Mozambican, much more so for a prisoner. But that is the love of Jesus that Tyren reflected so well—extravagant and full of mercy and grace.

Tiffany buried her husband and best friend in Mozambique. Then she returned to their home state of Connecticut with the children. She struggles daily with her grief and with how to move forward without Tyren by her side. Yet she continues to praise God and seek His face. I don't know what Ty's legacy will be, but I do know he and Tiffany have touched many hearts, including our own, with the love of Christ and an unshakable faith in Him. Please lift up Tiffany and the children in prayer for healing and the many difficult transitions they face in the years to come.

- Mendes, the vibrant young man who quoted Acts 2:17 and told us of his dream regarding the establishment of the church, passed away in the spring of 2016. Mendes was the son-in-law of Jon, the leader of the Chenganani house church. He was married to Jon's beautiful daughter Madelena and they had three young children. Mendes not only helped us to plant the church in Nomba, he and Madelena went on to serve with YWAM in Nampula. It was there that he complained of a severe headache one day. Within a matter of hours, he was paralyzed on one side of his body. Although he was rushed to the hospital, he died only twelve hours later.

Before that fateful day, Mendes appeared to be strong and healthy, in the prime of his life. His sudden death took a toll on all the church. For us, he was the third friend in Mozambique we lost in less than a year. It was a grim reminder of the difficulty of life there and the urgency of our work to know God and make Him known, to make the most of our fleeting time on earth. Yet the loss of our loved ones also causes me to long for a future time when "God Himself will be among [us] and He will wipe away every tear from [our] eyes; and there will no longer be any mourning, or crying or pain . . ." (Rev. 21:4).

May we live today for Him who laid down His life, so that we might have eternal life with Him. He knows suffering and He knows every tear we shed. As we draw near to Him in our grief, we receive the comfort only He can give.

- I was privileged to return to Mozambique in April of 2016, one year after we had left. Steve had started a new job and did not have enough vacation time to go, so I brought a team of three other ladies from our home congregation. It would be Brenda's third trip to Mozambique and a first for Sandra and Nansi. We were received with so much love. The house and grounds were immaculate. Miséria, Cascáo, and Merina had once again stocked our pantry full and prepared a welcome feast for us. Cascáo and Merina had a new baby daughter named "Soleil" (French for *Sun*), and they looked happy as ever. Miséria, in defiance of her name, looked radiant as well. We had a steady stream of visitors beginning with the chief who shared our welcome meal with us. Later, his wife and children came as well. When we weren't receiving visitors, we went visiting.

The church had been using our home as a base for the children's ministry, which meets three days a week. It was also used for the plant medicine ministry and the agriculture ministry. They had expanded my medicinal plant garden and my vegetable garden greatly. They also planted a church *machamba* on the adjoining land. Next to the cornfield they had planted peanuts. The *machmba* and vegetable garden were used for demonstrating agriculture techniques we referred to as "Farming God's Way." The produce was used to help widows, orphans, and others in the village experiencing hunger for various reasons, regardless of religion.

While we were there, we helped the church put on a four-day seminar held at our house for church members and seekers. My travel buddies taught the women's program, with me translating. We counted twenty-nine ladies from four different villages in attendance. The church leaders taught the men's program and the children's program, which were also well attended. Tabia and Isabella, fifteen years old, attended the children's program where they became convicted to follow Jesus. Shortly after our return, we learned they showed up the next Sunday wanting to be baptized. They were both the first members of their family to become Christian. Tabia is the daughter of the chief. While he did not give his blessing, he also did not forbid her, as most Muslim parents would have, and he did not throw her out of the home. It is a big step for this family who has much to lose (in a worldly sense) if they choose to follow Jesus.

The two house churches (Chenganani and Nomba) had doubled in size over the past year from twenty adult members to forty, despite the tragic death of Mariamo and Mendes. The Nomba church had grown outside the families of the original members, representing thirteen different families from three different villages. All the new believers were previously Muslim. It is truly an indigenous church. At the time of this writing (February 2017), both churches have grown considerably. We hear of groups of four or five new believers getting baptized every few weeks. I expect that by our next visit later this year, church membership will have doubled again. It is an exciting time.

When we worshipped with "the Love of Jesus" church on our last Sunday, I was so blessed deep down in my soul. Some of the new believers shared their testimony. Duana told us she was an alcoholic and used to abuse her family. They frequently went without food because she spent the money on alcohol. When she got drunk, she would yell and break things. Eventually, she became estranged from her family, who wanted nothing to do with her. In spite of that, church members began to reach out to her with God's word. They encouraged her to join them and learn about God. She began going on Friday nights to Miséria's house, and her heart was pricked. She gave her life to Christ, and He totally freed her from her addiction. Now she has her family back and her life back, as well as a good harvest of corn.

Next, a woman named Inez gave her testimony. Her daughter, Seuwa, had been participating in the children's program for several years. She would come home and tell her mother that the way they were living was not pleasing to God. This took great courage for Seuwa, now twelve, because in the Yao culture, even grown children do not speak against their parents. It also took great humility for Inez to listen to her daughter's counsel for the same reason, but she did listen. She decided to learn more for herself and joined the Friday night Bible study. Eventually, she became convicted that her daughter spoke the truth; they needed to follow Jesus no matter the cost. Mother and daughter were baptized together shortly before our arrival. Inez said that the neighbors make fun of her for following her daughter to a different religion. She said, "But now I no longer need my daughter to tell me right from wrong because I have the Holy Spirit living inside of me and He guides me."

After Inez finished her story, I shared a beautiful dream I'd had a month before our arrival. In the dream, I was singing and dancing with my team, worshiping God. I thought we were at our church in America. Then I heard two familiar voices singing in beautiful harmony, praising God in Chiyao. I looked over my right shoulder and saw Miséria and Asainabo singing and dancing. Beyond them were Cascão and Merina and the rest of the church. So I thought, "Oh, we are worshiping in Nomba, not in America." Then I looked farther back, and beyond the church members, I saw the chief and his family dancing and singing and praising God. And as I looked even farther back, I saw a whole multitude of Yao people worshipping God. That is when I realized that we were not in Nomba—we were all together in heaven.

They listened to my dream with great interest. The dream had encouraged me, and I believe it had the same effect on them. At the end of the service, church members circled around us and prayed over us. My team members were greatly moved by this gesture, just as I had been the year before.

The day before it was time to return to America, we went to the chief's house to say good-bye. At one point, the conversation turned to the plant medicine ministry. The chief's wife then called Tabia over and pointed to her ankle, saying, "Remember how well she healed?" The truth was I had all but forgotten until I saw the small scar on Tabia's right ankle.

It happened when we first came to the village, and we were still living in the Hampton's home. A woman had shown up at the house with a little girl. The child had an injury on her right ankle from falling off a bicycle several weeks prior. Although she had received treatment at the local hospital, the bone had become infected so that the wound would not heal. As was my custom, before I began treatment, I prayed to God for wisdom, healing, and for the child to know Jesus as her Savior.

Tabia's wound was one of the first injuries on which I used papaya. After cleaning the wound, I put a slice of the unripe fruit on it and bandaged it lightly. She returned every day with her mother and I changed the bandage until the wound was completely healed. The papaya did its work to remove all the dead tissue and she healed beautifully.

I had not been previously introduced to the woman and her child. That was before our current chief had become chief of Nomba. There was a different chief at that time who was very old and in poor health. He died a few months after our arrival, and only then did the current chief get appointed by the village elders.

My heart skipped a beat as I remembered and put the pieces of the story together. Only then did I realize how God had answered my prayer to heal Tabia and bring her to a saving faith. It seemed He was telling me not to worry; He would bring in the whole family soon. I marveled at how He hears *every* prayer and I silently thanked Him for His faithfulness. I considered all the children I had treated and prayed for in the previous five years. I regretted that I had not prayed even more!

I asked the family and my teammates to gather around as we offered up a corporate prayer of thanksgiving to God. We asked Him for His blessing and protection over this precious family and the village of Nomba. Before we left, Nansi was about to take a photo of me with the chief when he said, "Wait! I need to get something from the house first."

He came back with a photograph of me and Steve and held it up, next to his face. He said, "I want you to take the photograph with Steve in it, so he will know how much we miss him. We want him to come with you next time."

After leaving the chief's house, our final stop was Guida's house. She was very ill with severe headaches. She also had pain and bleeding from her eyes. She had lost weight and appeared to be in very poor health. It hurt to see her that way. I knew her former husband had died of AIDS, and I was concerned it might be the source of her illness. We laid hands on her and prayed for healing and restoration.

In stark contrast to Guida, the children looked great. Melody had already met us in the street and given me a big hug that spoke volumes. She was beaming when I asked her how her reading lessons were going. She took out her Bible and began to read from it. She read well. I was so thankful that Julio had kept his promise. I reminded Melody of her promise to teach her siblings. She said she had not forgotten and was already teaching them.

We had a wonderful visit, but I left with great concern for Guida's health. I asked the church leaders to continue to visit her and lift her up in prayer. I was relieved when I called her a few weeks after our return and learned that her health had been restored.

• Since our 2016 trip, Cascão and Merina were able to attend a three-month training program (sponsored by YWAM) near Quelimane. The focus of the program was church planting but they covered many other valuable topics as well, such as stewardship and accountability. I was glad they were able to take the opportunity to be fed and nourished spiritually, together as a family. They have continued to give every blessing they receive right back to God. Since their return to the village, Cascão continues to preach and shepherd the church. He also teaches the "Farming God's Way" program and leads Bible studies and evangelism campaigns.

He does this work in addition to his job and the work he does in his own *machamba* to provide for his family. He had never taken any compensation from the church until just recently when his hours at work were cut to part-time. His monthly wage went from $100/month to $57/month. The church leadership decided to make up the difference to help them get by. It was a big step in the right direction toward the maturation of the church. The church is still very poor in material wealth, but the time was right and there was a need. I was glad that they recognized and valued the sacrifices Cascão and Merina had made for the welfare of the church.

- Julio and Eugenia seemed to have worked through many of the difficulties they had early in their marriage, but they still need prayer. They have two children, Shonir and Resposta de Deus (Response from God). Julio has continued working in the children's ministry of the church, which is beginning to bear much fruit.

Recently two more young women, Lucia and Cecelia, have joined Seuwa, Tabia, and Isabella, in their decision to follow Jesus. A young man named Nildo was also baptized. As a child, Nildo was one of the first children enrolled in the orphan program in 2011. He was one of the more difficult children, and I had kicked him out of the program more than once for not obeying the rules. Because of his great need, however, each time I allowed him to re-enroll the following year. Please pray that the Lord will heal the wounds of his difficult childhood.

- Miséria and Asainabo attended the YWAM disciple training school (DTS) in 2016. There was not going to be a program they could attend in Lichinga that year, so they traveled to Nampula. Jon's other daughter, Rosa, and her husband, Arcango, from the Chenganani church, went with them. Victor and Lori Selemani had recently moved from Lichinga to Nampula to establish the new center there. Because of the Selamani's great love for the Lord, I was excited that Miséria and Asainabo would be attending DTS under their direction.

Miséria and Asainabo had a wonderful time at the school. During their practical time, Miséria got to travel to the Indian Ocean and witness to Muslim tribes there. She was so excited when she saw the ocean for the first time that she ran into the water and ruined her phone. It was some time before I was able to call her again.

Before the term ended, Miséria decided she could no longer tolerate the despair of her name. It did not fit her new life. She changed her name to Alegria (Joy), and she continues to radiate joy wherever she goes. In December of 2016, two of Alegria's prayers were answered when her grown daughters, Fatima and Margaret, chose to follow Jesus and were baptized. She continues to pray that her sons, Assumane, Samuel, and Bonifacio, will do likewise.

- After our return to the States in 2015, Steve went back to work. It was only with some difficulty that he was able to find a job. We don't know if the difficulty he had was because the manufacturing sector of the economy was slow, or because he was turning sixty, but he had to take a job away from home. Currently he is teaching machining technology at Texas State Technical College in Waco, a three-hour drive from our home. We only see each other on the weekends and are praying that he will get a transfer to a nearby campus soon, so that he can live at home.

Steve did not have enough vacation time to return to Mozambique in 2016, but we are hoping that he will be able to return with me by the end of this year. We plan to continue to visit yearly thereafter for as long as we are able. Even though we live apart, God continues to bless our marriage, keeping us on the same track. God has given us the gift of a united sense of purpose and love for the lost that guides us in every decision we make.

I have continued to stay in close contact with the church leaders (Cascão, Alegria, and Jon) since our departure. Sometimes I call others in the community that we were close to like the chief's family, Guida, and Lukia. I want them to know that we still care, and I also want to find out how the church is perceived in the eyes of the rest of the community. The chief's reports have been very positive and for that I praise God.

Now that I have finished recording the story of our journey, I plan to return to work part-time as a veterinarian. I want to leave myself plenty of freedom to work on behalf of the persecuted church and the billions of people around the world who do not have the light of Christ in their lives. Thank you for praying for them and for the church of the Yao.

Julie Henderson DVM

February 20, 2017

Guida and her younger children in 2016; Melody is holding her Bible.

O Lord, I ask for the power of your Spirit to adore you more fully.

Keep my spirit brightly infused by your Holy Spirit, O Lord, that thus energized,

My Lord, Jesus Christ and His perfections may be manifested in my mortal flesh.

O Lord, breathe on me until I am one with You in the temper of my mind and heart and disposition.

I turn to You.

How completely again I realize my lostness without You.

O Lord, I have no inkling of Your ways in external details, but I have the expectancy of Your wonders soon to be made visible.

Lord, I look to You.

How completely at rest I am, yet how free from seeing your way. You are God and I trust in You. [25]

Afterword

STEVE AND I WERE ABLE to return to Mozambique in December of 2017 as planned. It had been over two years since they had seen Steve and the joy at his return was great. When we worshipped on Sunday, the little pavilion was packed and many people had to sit outside.

The church had grown even more than we had expected with the combined membership of the two house churches reaching one hundred twenty-six, tripling since my visit in 2016. In addition to that, a church had been planted in the nearby village of Mitava, so some from that village who used to travel to Nomba to worship, like Nelito and Paulina, could now worship in their own village.

Immediately after worship, four more people were baptized that Sunday. We loaded as many as we could fit into our borrowed truck; others followed on motorcycles, and headed to the lake. I couldn't help but muse that we used to be able to fit the entire congregation in our truck when there was a baptism, now it was only a small fraction of the body.

Alegria and Ramos baptized the new believers: Samuel, Mantega, Celeste, and Jawado. Samuel is Alegria's middle son, another prayer answered. It was especially sweet to see an old man named Mantega come to know Jesus as Lord and Savior so near the end of his life. He had been homeless but was taken in by Fatima's family and shown the love of Christ. Fatima is Alegria's eldest daughter who came to Christ in 2016. In what has become their custom, onlookers to the baptisms joined the heavenly host in celebration—singing, dancing, and praising the Lord—as the new believers came up out of the water.

We returned to our house where the four-year anniversary celebration of the church was in full swing. The youth were in a big circle dancing to music powered by the generator, while the women worked to prepare a feast, and the men gathered under the veranda to visit one another. The chief and his wife, Rosa, were present to celebrate with us. Cascão had already related to us how the chief had come to the defense of the church on several occasions when leaders of the mosques had tried to stir up trouble against them. Apparently, the rapid growth of the church, and especially its appeal to the youth, was causing envy amongst the imams. They felt threatened that their position of power and influence in the community was diminishing. The chief, however, had convinced them to stand down each time by pointing out all the good the church had done for the entire community.

The chief himself is in a precarious position. He has been hearing the word of God for several years now, and I truly believe his heart's desire is to follow Jesus. His daughter, Tabia, is a strong believer and an active member of the church. More recently his wife has also expressed her desire to become Christian, but she is waiting on her husband. Should he make a public profession of faith in Christ, it is likely he will not only lose his position in the community but will also be severely persecuted so as to make an example. Please pray that he will fear God alone and have courage to follow his heart's desire for Jesus. As it so happened, the Lord provided Steve with three opportunities to strongly witness to the chief in a private setting during our visit. I think he was greatly encouraged by Steve's visit.

At one point in the celebration, Nildo came up to me and asked if I still had the photo I had taken of him the day he was admitted into the program. I went into the house and rummaged around. Much to my surprise, I found the stack of photos in a trunk. I used to study the photos to learn the children's names and faces and I used to pray over them to know Jesus. I looked through the stack until I came to Nildo's photo. It was such a sad photograph. There was no smile on his face, just a confused look. He was barefoot and covered in dust. His clothes were dirty and torn. I was almost reluctant to bring him the photograph, lest he be ashamed.

When I handed Nildo the photograph, he quickly snatched it from my hand and stared at the image, then held it to his chest. Overcome with emotion, he exclaimed, "Oh the poverty!" but could not finish his thought. After he composed himself, he began again, "Oh the poverty," he said in a quiet voice, "of a life without Jesus."

Nildo has indeed come to know Jesus. He was not ashamed of his rags, but rather he was overcome with joy by what the Lord has rescued him from. When it came time for us to say our good-byes, I left the stack of photos for Cascão to give to Nildo. Most of the rest of the children still do not know Jesus. I asked Cascão to remind Nildo of that fact and to encourage him to share his testimony with his friends. Please pray that Nildo will be faithful to do so, watering the seeds that were planted years ago.

Not all the news was good, however. Only a year after losing their son-in-law, Mendes, Jon and Carolina had recently lost their eldest son, James. He was on an evangelism outreach to an outlying village when he became sick with malaria and he died on the bus ride home. James left behind his pregnant wife, Telma, and their two young children. Telma is a new believer and her family has put great pressure on her to come home and revert back to Islam. She has stayed strong in the faith, however, and chosen to stay with her in-laws instead. Jon expressed his great sorrow, questioning God how this could happen while looking to Him for consolation at the same time. Please pray for this broken man who has been a stronghold for the Kingdom for so many years— the evil one attacks the strongholds.

Likewise, many in the small group of foreign missionaries to the Yao have suffered greatly and at least half of those we knew have left the field. The Paetzold family had worked in the village of Lucengewa about an hour's drive from Lichinga for many years. The first ten believers were baptized into Jesus early in 2017. The family went home to South Africa shortly thereafter to get some rest and medical care only to learn that the strange signs of muscle weakness and difficulty speaking that Alfred was experiencing were due to Motor Neuron Disease (aka ALS or Lou Gehrig's disease). The disease was progressing rapidly but they managed to return to Mozambique one last time to say good-bye to the people and home they loved. Despite their grief and pain, they too have clung to the Lord with a faith that is truly inspiring.

Jon and Cascão have continued to mentor the body of believers in Lucengewa, traveling there by motorcycle twice a month. We were eager to meet them and took a road trip with Jon, Cascão, and Alegria. By that time there were already fifteen believers and they seemed to be holding firm in their faith. Since we have returned from our trip we have learned that another four believers were baptized Easter Sunday and one of them was the leader of the local mosque. I am so glad that the Paetzold family has been able to witness the first fruits of their labor. Please hold them up in prayer as they walk through this difficult journey and pray for the church of Lucengewa to continue to grow strong in the faith.

Finally, I'll end on this good note. A few months after our return we were delighted to get a letter from Nelito and Paulina. They were the first family that Cascão discipled to Christ and he baptized them together in 2014, less than two years after his own baptism. They were the second family (after Cascão and Merina) who we sent to YWAM's Disciple Training School (DTS) that same year. In 2017 they served on staff at the DTS in Nampula with the Selemani family. It was during that time they felt God's call to the mission field. In the letter they told us of their plans to take their three young children and move to the village of Calolene in Sanga district, near the Tanzania border. They will go with another Christian family from Lichinga district as a missionary team. There they will plant a *machamba* and live with the people and share the Good News of Jesus Christ. There have been outreaches to the Sanga district but, as of yet, no church presence that I am aware of. The team hopes to plant a church that will plant more churches "to be the light for all of Sanga district." I feel certain that will happen.

God is good.

Julie Henderson, DVM

May 22, 2018

Visiting the chief's family in 2017, Tabia is standing next to me.

Bibliography

Chambers, Oswald. *My Utmost for His Highest.* Grand Rapids, MI, Discovery House, 1992.

Chambers, Oswald. *If You Will Ask.* Grand Rapids, MI, Discovery House, 1937.

Hanlon, Joseph. *Mozambique: The Revolution Under Fire.* London: Zed Books Ltd., 1984.

Russel, A.J. *God Calling.* Urichsville, OH, Barbour Publishing Inc., 1989.

www.ingramcontent.com/pod-product-compliance
Lightning Source LLC
Chambersburg PA
CBHW071206090426

42736CB00014B/2730